THE INTEGRAL LIFE

THE INTEGRAL LIFE

Complete Passion and Purpose for God

David A. Cross

TRILOGY
PROFESSIONAL PUBLISHING MEETS POWERFUL PROMOTION
A wholly owned subsidiary of TBN

The Integral Life: Complete Passion and Purpose for God

Trilogy Christian Publishers A Wholly Owned Subsidiary of Trinity Broadcasting Network

2442 Michelle Drive, Tustin, CA 92780

Manufactured in the United States of America

10 9 8 7 6 5 4 3 2 1

Library of Congress Cataloging-in-Publication Data is available.

ISBN: 978-1-68556-929-7

E-ISBN: 978-1-68556-930-3

Praise for "The Integral Life"

"In a world that overwhelms us with often-disconnected, fragmented information, it's seldom, even in Christian writing, to find a book that brings a holistic, cohesive approach to daily living. David Cross not only titles his book with the word 'integral,' but he points us to the pervasive, big-picture view of life lived in and through Scripture—from Genesis (made in God's image) to Revelation (glorified like Christ)—into all of life. David helps us answer not just the questions of who we are and why we exist, but also how to live in light of the who and why. Want to live a more-complete life? Read on!"

—Dr. Phil Norris
Professor of Music (ret.)
University of Northwestern—St. Paul

"Evangelicals have allowed systematic theology to break up our worldview into neat little packets of truth. In this book, David Cross gives the antidote to this fragmented view of our faith. He shows us the unity of the Bible's message and how its singular mission impacts us and our life mission."

—Ted Esler, Ph.D.
President
Missio Nexus

"*The Integral Life* is a breath of fresh air to the church. I love David Cross's missional approach to purposeful, complete discipleship. This work is sure to motivate every intentional Christ-follower in pursuing a kingdom dynamic in their life and the lives of all they impact."

—Will Ryan, Th.D.
Head of Biblical Studies and Theology
Covenant Theological Seminary

"We have been created for a purpose. In his book, *The Integral Life*, David Cross casts a vision for what a life oriented around a passion for God looks like. Sharing from his life and insights gathered along the journey, David takes on both lighthearted and weighty discussions. Through his reflections, David encourages us to set aside a compartmentalized view of life for the sake of embracing a bigger and more holistic view of a life lived on purpose before God. As a dear friend for over thirty years, I can attest to David's wise counsel and thoughtful reflections. As I have benefited from his friendship and wisdom, this book provides a pathway for many others to benefit from what I have treasured over the decades. May you join David in pursuing a complete passion and purpose for God."

—Justin Irving, Ph.D.
Professor of Leadership; Chair, Department of Leadership and
Discipleship Southern Evangelical Seminary

"An authentic and practical book about discovering one's Christian mission and calling in a world that competes for our passions. Engaging personal illustrations highlight David's own journey of listening to the voice of God in Scripture and being influenced by the heroes of the faith. His unique classification of Christians as creators, curators, and cultivators challenges the believer who is seeking to honor God in all aspects of life. All our work is sacred because we serve the Lord Jesus Christ!"

—Dr. Tim Kowalik, Ph.D
Professor Emeritus—Communication
University of Northwestern—St. Paul

ABOUT THE AUTHOR

David Cross is senior pastor of Riverwood Community Church in Burlington, Wisconsin, and founder and president of Professionals Global, an organization that mobilizes, equips, and mentors cross-cultural missionaries. He writes from over twenty years of cross-cultural missions experience, most of which were as a global professional in the Middle East and the United States. His passion for Scripture led him to obtain degrees in Bible and Biblical Studies from the University of Northwestern, Saint Paul, as well as a graduate degree in linguistics from the University of North Dakota. Cross is currently a doctoral student in Christian apologetics and culture at Trinity Seminary of Indiana.

Cross' previous works include *Work of Influence: Principles for Professionals from the Book of Daniel*, *Mondays in the Middle East: The Lighter Side of Arabian Nights* and contributor to *The Desert is Alive: Streams of Living Water from Muscat to Marrakech*. His hobbies include hiking and gardening with his wife and five children in Burlington, Wisconsin.

ACKNOWLEDGMENTS

In one sense, writing acknowledgments is a joy because I have the opportunity to recognize the valuable contributions many others have made to my life and my work. In another sense, I approach it with trepidation knowing that in my own frailty I will forget to note the key input of many people who have shaped my thinking. As with this entire book, those failings are my own, and I apologize in advance.

I am genuinely grateful to the Lord for his gentle care in showing me these insights into Scripture and life. My relationship with my Savior surpasses all other relationships, and it has been through this intimacy that I have learned these truths to pass on to others.

I am grateful to my wife, Cheryl, who not only helps me through those moments of searching for the perfect word or phrase, but she endures the moments of absent-mindedness when I drift off in conversation because of a mental "rabbit trail" in thinking over this book. She rejoices with me when those *eureka* moments fill my heart. Thank you, my "good gift."

Thank you to Stephen McKenzie who was the first person that I excitedly showed the *Telos Tower* to in our conversations in Starbucks. You were an excellent sounding board to shape these ideas.

Phil Norris, thank you for your decades of friendship and prayer. Your input on the first draft of the manuscript was invaluable and improved the work as a whole. You showed excitement over the impact of this book, and you've put it before others to get them energized as well. Thank you for your zeal for Scripture and excellence "*for glory and for beauty.*"

I am so thankful for my young friendship with Will Ryan and the kindred spirit we share not only for theology but for integrating all aspects of life to serve the Savior. Thank you for your willingness to share in this book and commend it to others.

I am grateful for friends who are willing to do what I cannot do. Linda Dzik, you helped me with the simple task of sharpening the look of the graphics in a way that I could not. Thank you for your aesthetic eye and willing heart.

Thank you to Shelbi Chandlee, Rhonda Webb, and the team at Trilogy Christian Publishing. I've felt like I am placing a newborn child in your hands by surrendering this book to you, and I feel like you've cared for it as you would a newborn child.

Thank you to you as you read this book as well. You've entrusted your time and energy to me. My hope and prayer is that the words in this book challenge your thinking and encourage your walk with the Lord. It is all for him.

—David Cross
2022

εἰς τὴν δόξαν τοῦ θεοῦ

DEDICATION

Dedicated to Dr. Kyle "Doc" Wilson whose integral life has served as a joyful model.

TABLE OF CONTENTS

FOREWORD

From the inception of the universe, humankind was created for a purpose. In the opening pages of the Bible, men and women were created with the intention to be set apart as a royal priesthood. That meant their job was originally to rule and reign, keeping and cultivating the sacred ways of the Lord God almighty devoted to intimate relationship with the him. The role of the royal priesthood is to bring the people of the world to the Lord and represent the Lord to the world as his ambassadors. The picture of this deep relationship with the Lord is described as walking together daily in the sacred space (cosmic temple) of the garden.

The Bible represents many things to many people, but at the heart of its divine purpose is to communicate that humankind is God's treasured possession and that he desires for deep intimate relationships with us. After the fall, things get far from the ideal plan or picture that God designed for us. But our continued calling as the royal priesthood is to be devoted to God's ideal plans and not get taken away by the things of the world. The plan of the world and Satan is to take what is holy and decimate and defile it. Satan's primary goal is to remove the purpose that you were designed for.

In Genesis 3:9, God asks what seems to be a strange question: "Where are you?" To understand exactly what is happening, we need to go back a chapter. In Genesis 2:15 we read, "Then the Lord God took the man and put him into the garden to cultivate it and keep it." The verb used is the Hebrew word ʿābad. This is the word we get our English word "abide" from. In Scripture we later see this reference applied to the Levitical priesthood in the forms of work, worship, and service. This represents the partnership that was given to Adam by God. When Adam and Eve fell, the partnership was compromised and the covenant was broken. Essentially, when God came looking for Adam in Genesis 3, he knew Adam had compromised his purpose. Shame is often the result of failed relationships. Adam realized that his relationship with God changed; he had become separated from the One who was the source of the meaning of his existence. He was no longer qualified to cultivate God's creation. Adam couldn't simply be forgiven; he needed to be reinstated.

"More grave than Adam's eating the forbidden fruit was his hiding from God after he had eaten it. 'Where art thou?' 'Where is man?' is the first question that occurs in the Bible. It is man's alibi that is our problem. It is man who hides, who flees, who has an alibi. God is less rare than we think; when we long for Him, His distance crumbles away" (Abraham Heschel, *Man Is Not Alone*, p. 153).

After Adam partakes of the fruit, we get the first question of the Bible: "Where is man?" As you begin this book, I invite you to ask the same question of yourself and your spiritual family. Where are you before the Lord? Who has God designed you to be? Through Christ (1 Peter 2:9) we are all reinstated to our original purpose and given specific gifts that will help us to function within the Body of Christ and his kingdom. What is God asking of you and how can you best use what you have been given to be the person that God created you to be.

I invite you to go on an amazing pursuit of personal purpose, finding your destiny within the kingdom of the Lord. David Cross has crafted a wonderful book to paint the picture that has the potential to help you not only create an incredible life, missional calling for yourself, but also for everyone you come in contact with. May you truly abide in him. We are invited to walk with God in the same partnership that was once given to Adam and Eve, and now in Christ, we have everything we need to be completely transformed and renewed and help others to also walk this path of purpose with the Lord.

Enjoy the stroll!

—Dr. Will Ryan
Head of Biblical Studies and Theology Department
Covenant Theological Seminary

INTRODUCTION

#CultureShockandAwe

What Hath God Wrought?

> *Surely there is no enchantment against Jacob, neither is there any divination against Israel: according to this time, it shall be said of Jacob and of Israel, "What hath God wrought!"*
>
> *Numbers 23:23 (KJV)*

"WHAT HATH GOD WROUGHT"

.-- .... .- - / .... .- - .... / --. --- -.. / .-- .-. --- ..- --. .... -

—the first words transmitted on the telegraph by Samuel F. B. Morse

Sparks. Electric shocks. Dry, dusty office buildings bursting into flame.

In the overnight hours of September 2, 1859, gold miners in the Rocky Mountains woke to the morning light and began to prepare breakfast. This rather ordinary event came with the rising sun every day in order to get a jump on the day and make the best use of the hours of daylight. There were no alarm clocks or shift whistles, but the work had to be done, so the miners were sensitive to the first break of dawn.

This ordinary event, however, would soon prove to be entirely out of the ordinary. The celestial anomaly that woke these miners started their day not at dawn, but midnight. Across the United States, the light of the *aurora borealis* enveloped the continent, causing fascinating and spectacular wonders in the heavens. People across New England were able to read newspapers unaided by candlelight. Others in the Caribbean, Mexico, and even as far south as Columbia shared how they enjoyed the intense, brilliant aurora of the so-called "Northern Lights." The *Baltimore American Commercial Advertiser* reported that the light of the aurora had been more brilliant than the full moon, but it covered the entire sky as a cloud.

As the night progressed into day, the sun's incredible coronal mass ejection (CME) that caused the nighttime display continued to stream toward Earth in the most powerful bombardment of these light-emitting particles on record, bringing unforeseen effects far beyond colorful night displays. In order to understand those effects, we need to step back some years to 1837, when Samuel Morse and his assistant, Alfred Vail, were putting the finishing touches on a working prototype of the telegraph.

In the ensuing months and years, Morse's telegraph and recording system would soon change the world of long-distance communication and thereby necessitate even more inventions such as Morse code, the telegraph key, and a switching network to make sense of incessant clicks and clacks coming out of the telegraph. Seven years later, in 1844, a proof of concept was ready for the national demonstration that would create the first communications infrastructure that would eventually span the world.

This demonstration transmitted a single phrase across forty-four miles of wire from the basement of the Supreme Court chamber in the U.S. Capitol building in Washington, D.C. to the Mount Clare Train Station in Baltimore, Maryland. The daughter of the U.S. Patent Commissioner, Annie Ellsworth, chose the simple phrase, and Samuel Morse transmitted, "WHAT HATH GOD WROUGHT." In this abbreviated quotation of Numbers 23:23, we find Annie Ellsworth's summation that though this creation was invented by Samuel Morse and Alfred Vail, it was nonetheless a reflection of God's creative gifts working in them both. Indeed, it was God's creation through them to change the world as we know it. The telegraph was not a claim of glory for themselves, but rather, Morse and Vail were rightly deferring the glory of their invention to the one who enabled them to create. Their artful creation was only due to God's work in them. *The Creator's image is in the creator.*

To be sure, Samuel Morse knew that his invention had incredible potential, but it is doubtful that even he could have foreseen the effect of his creation. He took the raw materials of wire, electricity, and electrical sparks at his disposal, and he made something far more useful to humanity as a whole. He created culture. From the moment of that successful demonstration of transmitting "WHAT HATH GOD WROUGHT," the world would never be the same, and everyone from that point forward would have the telegraph as part of their world, part of their culture.

Morse couldn't have known that his invention would be used to transmit wartime dispatches that would end thousands of lives and turn battles in one direction or another. He couldn't have known that within five years, his creation would conversely save many lives by enabling weather observations to give advance notice of life-threatening storms to whole regions. Morse couldn't have known that his creation would transmit news reports that would influence the outcome of political elections and change the course of American democracy through coast-to-coast news. He couldn't have known that the telegraph would be used to exchange money across the world and even prop up dictators in foreign lands or that it would be used to transmit such mundane messages as greetings from world travelers wishing to send dispatches to expectant family members back home. Yet, this is the world that Morse and Vail helped to create. Society as a whole crossed the Rubicon, a point of no return. Not only was there no turning back from the effects of the telegraph, but their invention itself would shape new culture in a world that would never be quite the same again.

Even with this unbounded success, the telegraph was not perfect, and there were cultural effects that would not have happened had the telegraph wires not been strung from city to city across the country. The cultural good of the telegraph needed input and innovations from others to become even more useful, and the CME of September 2, 1859, would show this only fifteen years after that famous message "WHAT HATH GOD WROUGHT."

The original design from Samuel Morse was an inexpensive, single-wire telegraph dependent on connections of wires to, in effect, make a single wire connecting city to city for communication across the country. In essence, these connections formed a wire thousands of miles long, which meant that the electrical signals could pass thousands of miles in an instant.

On the other hand, this wire that was thousands of miles long also became an antenna that was thousands of miles long that collected the cosmic radio energy across the span of the entire country. On September 3, 1859, the normally placid effects of that energy exploded in force as the Earth turned to face the full strength of the massive solar storm. The electrical energy from the sun's coronal mass ejection (CME) was collected by this extremely long and efficient antenna.

The cumulative force was transmitted across the length of the wire to the endpoints where it burst forth, effectively sending lightning shooting out of the telegraph keys. Operators across the country were knocked out of their chairs by these intense jolts of electricity. Some of these shocks were so powerful that they sent sparks shooting out of the systems, which triggered fires in the wooden telegraph offices and burned entire office buildings to the ground. Other milder effects after the initial surges energized the entire telegraph network over the following days, allowing operators to continue to transmit and receive messages with no power to the system.

Indeed, even with all of the information that Morse had accumulated and developed in his invention, there was a great deal yet to be learned. As an example of the cultural mandate given by God, culture is added to culture. Morse created a cultural good, and others who followed him would add to that cultural good, making new culture.

Morse took the materials and knowledge he had and created a cultural good more useful for the world. His invention brought regions, nations, and the world under the dominion of humankind. In this way, the example of the telegraph is, to be sure, a demonstration of the original command from God given to the first man and woman.

The Integral Life follows the path of human culture from that point of the original command forward. To this end, the book is laid out in the following three sections:

Section One introduces the context of being created in the image of God. This context is laid from the *cultural mandate*, which is given in Genesis 1 and 2. Being made in the image of God specifically identifies us as *creators*, *curators*, and *cultivators*, just as God showed himself to be. In the cultural mandate, we are given work, which is a good and honorable thing. This work is characterized as *art*, *order*, and *care* as the work that God did in *creation*.

The edifice of work with its intrinsic value is used as a model to illustrate radical interdependence that we have on one another in all of the moral work done in society. By way of contrast, *radical independence* and *radical dependence* are shown to be incomplete in describing the biblical picture of relationship to God and to one another. Radical interdependence, then, becomes the model of our lives as members of the Body of Christ.

In Section Two, this radical interdependence is demonstrated to be our means of relationship in other domains of life. Not only do we manifest the image of God when we work dutifully, but we express the created design of radical interdependence in other domains of life such as friendship, marriage, parenting, and the life of the Church itself.

Finally, Section Three concludes with the application of that context to our specific role of representing God across the globe through missions and evangelism. Additionally, Section Three looks at the limits of missions and evangelism, specifically, the terminal limit when we will no longer do missions and evangelism. We set a course for understanding our continued role in relationship to God in the last days on this earth and our eternal presence with the Savior in the New Heavens and New Earth.

Regarding this approach that encapsulates all of life, it is worth noting at the outset that this is a different approach than the Seven Mountains approach engendered by Bill Bright and Loren Cunningham. To differentiate *The Integral Life* from the Seven Mountains, it might help to share a bit of history of the Seven Mountains' approach to society.

In 1975, Bill Bright (founder of Campus Crusade) and Loren Cunningham (founder of Youth With A Mission) envisioned needed change in all of society. To effect that change, they identified seven spheres or seven "mountains" of society that needed to be claimed and transformed for Christ. Those Seven Mountains are religion, family, education, government, media, arts and entertainment, and business.

To be sure, these are worthy goals, and much good has come from aiming to transform these spheres of society. On the other hand, these Seven Mountains do not reflect the type of whole-life living envisioned in *The Integral Life*.

One of the most obvious differences between Seven Mountains and *The Integral Life* is that Seven Mountains sees religion and spirituality as separate from other spheres of life like business or education or government. As we will see throughout the current book, *The Integral Life* sees all of these spheres as part of the natural outworking of faithfully following God. These pursuits are ordained as an outworking of our religious practice as we fulfill the creation mandate given in the first chapters of Genesis.

Much explanation is required to elucidate the differences in these two approaches, but suffice it to say at this point that *The Integral Life* is not Seven Mountains repackaged in different wrapping paper. *The Integral Life* is a distinct call for all believers to live out the cultural mandate and, in so doing, to reach the world with the Gospel.

In conclusion, then, the path is set forth for us to invest in the intrinsic value of the work we do, knowing that it manifests our created design. Whatever moral work we engage in, we are engaging neither less nor more in "sacred" work than a pastor, missionary, or full-time Christian worker. Indeed, all aspects of our lives are equally honoring to God because of our intent to do them for his glory, and all of those aspects of our time on earth serve the purpose of preparing us for eternity with our Savior. In this way, our time on earth is not the focal point of our existence, but rather, it is simply a preparation to build the capacity to glorify God and to enjoy our Creator forever.

May these words spur you on toward a whole, complete, integral life. May you know the joy of serving the Lord in all you do. May your service and joy in the Lord brightly reflect the image of God within you as you engage in complete passion and purpose for God.

May this book be εἰς τὴν δόξαν τοῦ θεοῦ (*eis ten doxan tou theou* "To the glory of God").

—David A. Cross

SECTION I–THE TWO TOWERS

In the evangelical world, we have the tendency to simmer the message of the Bible until only the salient points of the Gospel remain:

- Humans sinned.
- God sent his Son as a perfect sacrifice to remove sin.
- Jesus' death and resurrection showed victory over sin.
- Those who trust in Jesus will live with him forever.

This is our minimalistic approach to the Gospel, and it makes sense as *evangelicals* because we want to know what the minimum requirements are for *evangelism*. What are we required to share for evangelism and what is someone required to believe to be a genuine believer in the Gospel?

To be clear, I love minimalist thinking and minimalist behavior. I enjoy removing all distractions from my desk, for example, so that I can efficiently operate with minimal implements for writing. Minimalism in the Gospel, however, doesn't serve us as we might expect. It would be like asking, "What is the minimum number of bites required to enjoy a feast?" If it's a feast, I don't want the minimum. I want to enjoy all of the feast!

In this effort at identifying the minimal elements of the Gospel, the context of the Gospel in relation to God's work through his people is boiled away. Our efforts at minimalism are good because we identify what is absolutely essential, but, on the other hand, we shouldn't forego the feast! We need to see the Gospel in light of all God has for his people throughout the Bible.

Without realizing it, our trek through Scripture has become more of a triple jump rather than running a 1600-meter race. We jump from the first chapters of Genesis to Matthew to Revelation. Our minimalist approach to the salvation message leaves us with a minimal understanding of Jesus as King, a minimal understanding of God's work through his people, and a minimal understanding of God's engagement in the totality of our lives. With this starting place, it is no wonder that so many believers who have accepted this minimalist Gospel give God only minimal reign over their lives.

The following section fills out the picture for us with God's intent and plan for his people from the very beginning. By seeing his plan in this light, we get the full perspective of the entire Bible. We get the perspective of the prophets and Jesus and the Apostles, and we get the perspective planned for believers since the completion of the New Testament.

The escape from a minimalist view of Scripture necessitates a return to the foundation of Scripture and what God has done in and through his people. To accomplish that, it is incumbent to start at the beginning. Even before doing that, however, we draw near the beginning to demonstrate the contrast between two towers of mutiny and majesty.

CHAPTER I–THE TOWER OF BABEL: MUTINY

#LestWeBeScattered

In 1719, Bartholomew Roberts was an unassuming navigator aboard *The Princess,* where he had made numerous trips across the North Atlantic. Nonetheless, Roberts was about to enter infamy in a manner largely out of his control.

On June 6, *The Princess* was overrun and captured by pirates. As was often the case with piracy, the crew who survived the capture were given a choice. The first option was to die a noble death immediately at the hands of the victorious pirates. The second option was to join the ignoble life of pirates and put the skills of their trade into the employ of buccaneers on the open waters.

Bartholomew considered these options and came to the following conclusion, "If a pirate I must be, 'tis better being a commander than a common man."[1] His decision was made. He was to be a pirate. More than that, Bartholomew Roberts, or "Black Bart," would become the most successful pirate in history in his short few years.

Nevertheless, it is remarkable to note the code of conduct that Black Bart enforced aboard his vessels. To begin, he maintained

1 Richard Sanders, *If a Pirate I Must Be… The True Story of "Black Bart," King of the Caribbean Pirates* (New York, NY: Skyhorse, 2007), 57.

the personal standard of never drinking alcohol despite capturing extreme quantities of rum aboard seized vessels. He added the personal standard of never going ashore when his ships entered port even though his crew took advantage of the opportunity to carouse in licentiousness.[2] He even maintained principles among his crew to ensure the respectful care of women aboard the ships he claimed as prizes.

The common view of piracy is that it is a world of lawless, raiding marauders with no respect for life or property, but in actual fact, pirates often bound themselves to their other crewmates by signed charters. Black Bart even expressed the culture of piracy with a provision for drinking plundered rum, stating that each man "has equal title to the fresh provisions or strong liquors at any time seized, and may use them at pleasure unless a scarcity makes it necessary for the food of all to vote a retrenchment."[3]

Despite this pirate culture, there was one act whose participants were given no quarter, even among pirates: mutiny. Uncivilized pirates relied on mutual trust and interdependence for their racket to work, so the betrayal of mutiny was shown no mercy, and its punishment was a horrific death. Even within the ignobility of piracy, mutiny severed trust too violently for repair.

Mutiny on the Plains

Many people are familiar with the Tower of Babel, which is detailed eleven chapters into the Bible, specifically because this tower is the point at which the Lord introduced different languages to humankind. Of course, those languages deeply affect

2 Little, Benerson. *The Golden Age of Piracy.* (New York: Skyhorse Publishing, 2016), 110.

3 Curtis, Wayne. *And a Bottle of Rum: A History of the New World in Ten Cocktails.* (New York: Crown Publishing, 2018), 43.

every person on earth, so the scope of this famed story is immense in its impact. That being said, this story is more than just the introduction of languages, and it will be a great help to look at the text itself to see it in its entirety:

> *The whole earth had a common language and a common vocabulary. When the people moved eastward, they found a plain in Shinar and settled there. Then they said to one another, "Come, let's make bricks and bake them thoroughly." (They had brick instead of stone and tar instead of mortar.) Then they said, "Come, let's build ourselves a city and a tower with its top in the heavens so that we may make a name for ourselves. Otherwise we will be scattered across the face of the entire earth."*
>
> *But the Lord came down to see the city and the tower that the people had started building. And the Lord said, "If as one people all sharing a common language they have begun to do this, then nothing they plan to do will be beyond them. Come, let's go down and confuse their language so they won't be able to understand each other."*
>
> *So the Lord scattered them from there across the face of the entire earth, and they stopped building the city. That is why its name was called Babel—because there the Lord confused the language of the entire world, and from there the Lord scattered them across the face of the entire earth.*
>
> *Genesis 11:1–*

We should not underestimate the gravity and impact of what is done in these few verses. As noted previously, the introduction of various languages is ubiquitous in its impact touching every person in every place in all epochs. Even so, consider what the people of Babel were proposing in light of what God had commanded humans to do in the first chapter of Genesis,

> *God created humankind in his own image, in the image of God he created them, male and female he created them.*
>
> *God blessed them and said to them, "Be fruitful and multiply! Fill the earth and subdue it! Rule over the fish of the sea and the birds of the air and every creature that moves on the ground."*
>
> *Genesis 1:27*

First, people were made in God's image. They were created to reflect the greatness of God's glory. Everywhere they went, people would display the greatness of God by showing his image, which would give him supreme glory.

Second, they were given the command to multiply and to go throughout the earth. In so doing, they would carry the greatness of God's image throughout all the earth.

Now, look once again at what the people of Babel did and consider it in light of what God commanded. First, they migrated to the plain of Shinar "*and settled there.*" They were commanded to fill the earth, but instead, they settled. This is the first act of disobedience that we see in the text. This might seem incidental, and it might seem that too much is being made of a simple word or two, but consider the people's words themselves and how they expressly identify their own sin:

> *"Come, let's build ourselves a city and a tower... Otherwise we will be scattered across the face of the entire earth."*

Their intent might not seem obvious to us, but it was certainly obvious to them and to the first readers of the book of Genesis. The people were engaging in rebellion. The intent of their heart was mutiny. Settling in the plain of Shinar was not simply working with a realtor to buy a nice piece of property in a good neighborhood. These people knew what their actions meant to God, and they knew what it meant for them. They did not want to obey God's command. They did not want to "*be scattered across the face of the entire earth.*" They were disobeying God's command, and this act of defiance betrayed any masked intention.

> *Secondly, consider what their actions signaled: "We may make a name for ourselves."*

Again, we might not see the nuances of their actions at first glance, but these people knew what their actions signaled. Their intent was to make a name for themselves rather than making a name for God and the glory of his name.

Building a tower, which reached into the heavens, served as a response by the people of Babel to thwart God's ability to destroy humankind again through a flood. The existence of a tower would be a snub to God, effectively saying, "You don't have power over us. We can save ourselves from your actions to destroy us because we have this tower."

This scene of a mortal game of *King of the Mountain* and *Lord of the Flies* certainly fits the depravity of humanity but likely would have resulted in the destruction of humankind anyway. Given the paucity of the population that would be saved at the top of such a tower, it seems that saving those people is a less-likely explanation than the ideological and/or physical explanation that the people desired to take the place of God himself. In fact, both are possible. Their aim was to unseat God from his heavenly throne by building a tower "*with its top in the heavens.*" Additionally, this would show that they believed they were superior to God by being able to withstand another flood.

The very next phrase in the text shows their true colors: "*So that we may make a name for ourselves.*" This was a declaration of war against their Maker. The people of Babel wanted to make a name for themselves that was superior to God's name, and they acted in light of that belief expecting that they could unseat God from his heavenly throne by building a tower to reach heaven itself.

This, then, is our first tower, the Tower of Babel. The actions of Genesis 11 describe rebellion, mutiny, and extreme hubris. Believing that they were superior to the Creator himself, the people of Babel directly refused to obey God's commands, did not honor him with their obeisance, declared war against God, and fully intended to dethrone him so that their name alone would be worshiped on the earth.

CHAPTER 2–THE TELOS TOWER: MAJESTY

#OnMissionInMissions

Philip said, "Lord, show us the Father, and we will be content." (John 14:8.)

Swinging the Pendulum

In contrast to the Tower of Babel, I want to describe another tower that I will call the *Telos Tower*. *Telos* (*tell'-aws*) is the Greek word describing an end, or a purpose, or a goal. You might recognize this word as the first part of *tele-scope* through which an astronomer looks to the end.

The Telos Tower, then, is not a physical tower but rather a conceptual onc. The building blocks of the Telos Tower are the various concepts and teachings from Scripture that identify our human purpose. Considering that the Telos Tower marks our path and purpose from the very beginning, we need to uncover its roots from the very beginning of Scripture in Genesis.

Starting at the Beginning

To get to an understanding of the Telos Tower, we need to start at the beginning, and that takes us back to Genesis 1. As we journey back on this trek through Scripture, keep in mind that the account of Creation was not written from an eyewitness perspective. Moses was the human author of this book of Scripture, but he was not watching the act of Creation unfold before him so that he could record it for our benefit. In fact, Moses did not witness anything we read in the fifty chapters of Genesis. Rather, all of it was passed down to him through extensive oral tradition. We believe and trust that as the story was passed on from Creation through the story of Joseph in Egypt that it was safeguarded by the Lord. We trust that the accuracy of the account was protected by God, who was himself the only eyewitness of Creation in the first place.

After all, Moses notes that "*the Lord would speak to Moses face to face, the way a person speaks to a friend*" (Exodus 33:11), so we can understand that the Lord confirmed what had been passed through oral tradition. Everything else had a beginning, but only God exists through all of eternity, so only he could relay the accurate account of Creation for the benefit of his creatures. The words used in the narrative are precisely the words that God wanted to use in order to relay to people everything he intended.

That being understood, one of the key points we need to recognize about God is his identity as Creator. There is only one God who made everything from nothing. Throughout Scripture, we find passages like Acts 17:24

> *The God who made the world and everything in it, who is Lord of heaven and earth, does not live in temples made by human hands, nor is he served by human hands, as if he needed anything, because he himself gives life and breath and everything to everyone.*

Because he created it, he is Lord over it. When we read through Genesis 1 and each part of the Creation story that the light was good and the dry land and seas were good and that the vegetation was good and the stars were good and the birds and fish were good and that the land animals were good—God gets glory. His glory is preeminent over all things. God's glory is, first and foremost, the reason for Creation. This is the foundation of the Telos Tower.

Understanding that, we can move forward with the next layer of the Telos Tower, namely, why are humans here?

Why Are You Here?

As a teenager, I loved science and, specifically, physics. Fortunately for me, my homeroom teacher, Mr. Gephardt, was the physics teacher of my high school. This meant that I had access to all sorts of physics equipment even before I was permitted to take advanced physics as a class in my senior year of high school. By that point, I had been allowed to build a number of projects, such as a hoverboard that seated passengers could ride across the gymnasium floor while levitating millimeters above the surface of the floor.

Even so, much of the more expensive equipment was held back from me, and it was only allowed to be used by students of advanced physics so that it wouldn't be damaged. This included the Van de Graaff generator, which would create lightning in the classroom or make your hair stand on end. The school's laser stayed locked up as well, despite my many pleadings to be allowed to fire its red beam through a maze of mirrors scattered through the third-floor hallways of Goodrich High School. This was long before lasers were commonplace as laser pointers in people's pockets. The $500 laser was a serious piece of equipment that enamored all of us to see in person.

The laser itself is a fascinating invention that came out of AT&T's Bell Labs. Bell Labs was an incredible innovation where, from 1925, they gobbled up the best and the brightest from America's university science graduates and funded them to simply do their thing. Experiments, equipment, and assistants were all paid for so that these scientists could produce the next best wonder that would advance Bell Telephones in human innovation.

Bell Labs became a casualty of the breakup of Ma Bell, but up to that point, some remarkable inventions came out of this think tank. Chief among these inventions were undoubtedly the transistor and the laser. One fueled the digital age, and the other stirs kittens everywhere into paroxysms of joy. It wouldn't be an exaggeration to note that the laser even helped drive the USSR toward bankruptcy as the country emptied its coffers to match Ronald Reagan's supposed Star Wars. The ubiquity of these inventions has proven so financially successful that they easily could have funded Bell Labs in perpetuity. Still, in 1925 at the inception of Bell Labs, who could have possibly seen this coming? Could anyone have predicted that Bell Labs would invent the transistor? In 1925, could those who started Bell Labs have envisioned the transistor replacing the vacuum tube and miniaturizing unthinkable computing power into the palm of one's hand? Could anyone have known that the laser would come out of Bell Labs and be one of the most ubiquitous, versatile inventions of the twentieth century?

Even now, we are amazed at Christmas laser light shows that we can see clearly only because of Lasik surgery. We stand in awe at the computational power of computers that have beaten humans at Jeopardy, chess, and Go with today's computer chips that pack in 2.6 billion transistors each. We see the glorious beauty and simplicity and function of these inventions, but no one would have guessed where we would be today when Bell Labs was started nearly a hundred years ago.

The fact is, though, Bell Labs was not started to invent the transistor. Those scientists were not hired with the expectation that they create a laser. Nonetheless, those scientists did what they were trained to do and what they were made to do.

The Telos Tower is the mother of all Bell Labs. It is the place where we see why we are here, and that "why" gives life meaning. The Telos Tower explains our insatiable love of order and beauty and creativity, from architecture to music to fractals with infinite perimeter. It is the place where we find meaning and purpose in work, marriage, family, friendship, Church, and community. The Telos Tower wraps all of these domains of life into one integral life of service and worship of the Creator.

Set Apart from the Moment We Were Put Together

Genesis begins with what is called the pre-Creation account just before humans are created, where God says (1:26–27),

> *Then God said, "Let us make humankind in our image, after our likeness, so they may rule over the fish of the sea and the birds of the air, over the cattle, and over all the earth, and over all the creatures that move on the earth."*
> *God created humankind in his own image, in the image of God he created them, male and female he created them.*

So, we are all created in the image and likeness of God. Jonathan

Edwards says of this creation,

> *He brought a physical reality into existence in order that it might experience his glory and be filled with it and reflect it—every atom, every second, every part and moment of creation. He made human beings in his own image to reflect his glory, and he placed them in a perfect environment which also reflected it."*[4]
>
> *Cited in Alcorn, Heaven, 226*

He didn't make any other animals in his image or in his likeness. That fact sets us apart from all other animals, but what exactly does it mean to bear the image and likeness of God?

Clearly, we are different from other animals. For example, we have an innate capacity for reason and for language that cannot be explained in its difference from other animals. Even now, scientists are unable to define consciousness—something we inherently understand as humans. We have a notion of time that no other being in Creation shares. We can describe emotions we felt last week when no other animal can understand the notion of time, much less a description of feelings in time. We are different.

Genesis 1 gives a purpose statement of why we are created differently from everything else: "*So they may rule.*" That purpose clause may answer why God did what he did, but we have to ask, what does it mean that we are created in the image and likeness of God? What had God done or shown in his character in the Creation story that we should model or reflect to be in his image or likeness?

4 Alcorn, Randy. *Heaven.* (Carol Stream, Illinois: Tyndale House Publishers, 2004), 226.

In answering this, we can see that there are some actions and attributes of God that we simply cannot mimic because we are not God. For example, God showed himself to be supreme and preeminent over all things because all things came into being through him. By that measure, he is not restricted in his strength, presence, or by time. He obviously created all energy, so he is greater than the sum of all energy and power. He created the dimensions of space, so he is outside of those dimensions and cannot be confined by them. Finally, with time being the sequential ordering of events traced to the moment of Creation, God cannot be limited by time since he created matter and the beginning of those events.

These attributes of God make sense to the theologian and philosopher who have a wide understanding of science, but they don't seem to fully address the simple nature of the author's intent in saying we are created in the image and likeness of God. Rather, it seems that Moses intended Genesis to be read and understood by everyday people, so everyday people should be able to grasp its meaning with the words that are there. Fortunately for us, the concept of the image of God is readily accessible through the immediate context.

So, again we ask, up to this point in the story, what had God done? What had he revealed about his nature? What showed the image and likeness of God?

The answers to these questions show three characteristics of what God did that we model. These three characteristics are the bricks of the next layer of the Telos Tower. They show the image of God that we were to exhibit and display.

The first and most obvious act is the creation of something from nothing. God did that, and it is reasonable to understand that we should do something like *create* if we reflect the character and nature of God. To be sure, we cannot create the elements of the world such as he did, but we take those elements he made and create things and ideas that are more than they would have been without our creation. We call this *art*. Where there was nothing, we fashion something useful and beautiful. God is the Creator. Like God, we are creators.

Second, God did not just create all things and leave them in an untamed, chaotic state. Rather, he brought order from disorder and put the planets and stars into motion by which we might measure time. Our sense of time being past, present, and future is something the rest of the animal kingdom does not have. Those are the most rudimentary concepts of time, yet only humans have them. Of course, our concept of time is far more replete with the sense of millennia, centuries, decades, years, months, weeks, days, hours, minutes, seconds, nanoseconds, picoseconds, etc. Our sense of time shows an extreme inclination toward the ordering of events. Indeed, even with such advanced concepts of Einstein's theories of relativity, we observe both the sequential ordering of events and the relation of objects to one another in space, and this is all an aspect of order that models God's order of all things.

God brought order from disorder through time, and he brought order from disorder through our sense of space. On earth itself, he gathered the sky into one place, the waters into another place, and the land into a place separate from the waters. Space makes sense only in the relationship of objects to each other throughout the universe. By putting these boundaries into place, God curated order from disorder.

In a similar manner, when we bring order to the raw materials we are given, we make something more useful and beneficial for growth than it would have been as untamed wilderness. We exercise our innate inclination to order. God is a Curator. Like God, we are curators.

Finally, God provided all that is needed to survive and thrive on earth. Indeed, in the retelling of the Creation story with deeper detail in Genesis 2, God himself planted a garden. He did not merely drop humans into a desert or into a thicket in the wilderness, wishing them the best of luck. He expressed care for us by providing all we needed to eat and be healthy and flourish and grow. As a matter of fact, God himself visited the first humans to check on their growth, health, and well-being. He managed the growth, or culture, of his Creation, and when we cultivate growth, we reflect his image and likeness. Indeed, the culture we ourselves exhibit manifests the growth we see in all civilization. God is a Cultivator. Like God, we are cultivators.

In summary, where at first there was nothing, and we make something useful and beautiful, we show ourselves to be creators just as God is the Creator. When we bring order from disorder, we show ourselves to be curators of what God has given us, and we model his image and likeness of a Curator. Finally, when we foster an environment for growth or culture, we show ourselves to be cultivators, just as God is a Cultivator.

Though we may reflect the image and likeness of God in many other ways, at the very least, we are creators, curators, and cultivators. These three roles reflect the art, order, and care we see in the character and nature of God and that we bear in our own nature being created in the image of God.

A Purpose-Driven Existence

In my personal story, I needed purpose. It was the search for meaning and purpose that drove me to God. I needed to know what gave life meaning for the five days of the week instead of the two days of hedonism on the weekend. I needed to know what my purpose was from the Creator's perspective. What on earth was I here for? Further, as a follower of God, I had to ask, "What is the mission of God's people?"

It is this exploration of the mission of God's people that leads to some of life's most central questions. What are we here for? Why were we created? What are we supposed to do with our lives? How does our purpose affect marriage, society, and even our jobs? What will we do after this life? How do our actions draw us near to our Creator?

We might even put this into the contemporary term of "mission." However, it is critical to note that the word "mission" has two meanings. The lexical definition of "mission" has these two pertinent senses: first as a "calling or vocation" and second as "a specific task with which a person or group is charged."[5]

First, mission is an overarching purpose, aim, calling, or goal. The analogy of a war might be useful to illustrate this. During the first Iraq War, the mission was to liberate Kuwait from the oppression of Saddam Hussein and his Iraqi government that had seized control of another sovereign country. Once that mission was accomplished, the war was over.

In the midst of this, though, the soldiers and pilots and sailors and intelligence officers of the United States carried out myriad missions. These missions were smaller activities that contributed to accomplishing the larger goal. These activities included the most fearsome tank battle in all of history. These missions included sortie after sortie of pilots dropping bombs to subdue the Iraqi government into releasing its hold of Kuwait. So, it is clear: people were sent on many missions to accomplish the mission of freeing Kuwait.

This analogy is important because several contemporary authors

5 "Mission," Merriam Webster, accessed April 22, 2022, https://www.merriam-webster.com/dictionary/mission.

have fallen into the error of conflating the two senses or simply ignoring one or placing one sense over the other. This has resulted in general confusion for readers. Books like *When Everything Is Missions* and *What Is the Mission of the Church?* present opposing views. The first is mistaken because it ignores a primary sense of "mission" in its definitions. The second is mistaken because it defines the question so narrowly that it is no longer the question people are asking.

To address this, a further point of confusion worth resolving is that there are distinct differences between the mission of God, the mission of people, the mission of God's people, the mission of Jesus, the mission of the Church, and missional ministry. With each of them, we can ask, "What is the purpose being accomplished?" Also, we must ask, "Who is being sent?" and "What are they sent to do?"

For example, we can look at the redemptive work of Jesus. What is the purpose being accomplished here? The purpose of God's redemptive work through Jesus is to redeem believers from the clutches of sin.

Who is being sent? Jesus was one person sent, but there were others sent. What was Jesus sent to do? In God's sovereignty, Jesus was sent with the mission of dying and rising again in victory over death. However, we could add that, in God's sovereignty, Pontius Pilate was "sent" with the mission of crucifying Jesus. We could add that Caiaphas was "sent" to be a hard-hearted high priest who would refuse to be moved by Jesus' many miracles and teachings. He was sent with the ultimate mission of pursuing Jesus to crucifixion.

So, there are many missions to accomplish one mission. The deep flaw of *When Everything Is Missions* is that it does nothing to recognize these two facets of "mission." Because of this, it is shortsighted and dangerous because it misleads people to conclusions based on just one meaning of the terms mission and missions. Indeed, it can lead people to completing mission activities with the belief that they have accomplished the mission. To return to our war-time analogy, this would be akin to a pilot successfully completing a sortie and thinking the war has now been won.

In this way, today's confusion over missions illegitimately makes the activity into the goal. As we will see later, the specific example of missions will end (that is, evangelizing "*every tribe, language, people, and nation*"), but the mission of God's people will continue.

In a similar manner, the accomplishment of completing those missions might be an activity for a larger, umbrella mission. We can continue to consider the death and resurrection of Jesus to see this. Even though his death and resurrection were the aim or mission for Jesus coming to earth, they were but one part of God's mission for all of humanity. That mission or aim for all humanity certainly includes the death and resurrection of the Messiah and the ensuing faith of believers for salvation, but it also includes the mission for humanity before humankind needed redemption. It even includes the mission for those believers after the consummation of their salvation in the New Heavens and New Earth. The redemption of believers into eternal salvation is itself under a larger mission for humankind, and that mission for humankind is under the larger mission of God to bring glory to himself. It simply is not sufficient to define only the mission of the Church, for example, without considering the mission of God's people. And it is not sufficient to define the mission of God's people without defining the mission of humankind.

"Nothing Sucks Like an Electrolux"[6]

Slogans are so tempting because they can be catchy and memorable. A popular slogan in Sweden for the Electrolux vacuum cleaner was "Nothing Sucks Like Electrolux." Of course, this slogan means something quite different to English speakers in Europe than it does to those in the US.

Basing a whole argument on a slogan is dangerous because a slogan, by definition, leaves out quite a lot of information. Slogans run the particular risk of leaving out information pertinent to the proposition of the slogan itself.

One such slogan that is getting a lot of mileage is, "If everything is mission, nothing is mission," by Stephen Neill. Given that Stephen Neill was a career missionary, we can understand the meaning of this claim to be: if every action in our lives is classified as "mission," then there is no defining characteristic to set apart mission activities (read: *cross-cultural evangelistic activities*) from other activities. For Neill, classifying clean water projects, agricultural development to feed the poor, and rescuing prostitutes as "mission" was a personal affront to his life's work of evangelism which is what he considered to be "mission." Others, too, have latched on to this slogan in presumably well-meaning attempts to defend missions (again, read: *cross-cultural evangelism*).

That being the meaning of the slogan, there are two major errors of the slogan. First, it fails to define "mission" in light of the other "missions." Indeed, it fails to define any other "missions." Which mission is being discussed? Are we speaking of the mission of God, the mission of people, the mission of God's people, the mission of the Church, or the mission of Pontius Pilate? De-

---

6 Nothing Sucks Like an Electrolux—Billboard UK 1991. Adland®. (2021, February 10). Retrieved October 4, 2022, from https://adland.tv/ooh/nothing-sucks-electrolux-billboard-uk-1991

pending on that answer, it is necessary to view "mission" in light of the other missions enumerated above.

Second, the slogan conflates the two senses of mission into one. Mission as a purpose or aim is lumped in with the mission activity of sending people to accomplish something to support the purpose or aim. Without defining "mission" in light of the many other missions, we haven't defined "missions" at all. Rather, we've made the waters murky and the words more confusing because of this slogan.

The Pagan Source of Confusion in Missions

This confusion reflects a startling and undesired source of thought. Defining "missions" exclusively as evangelization reflects an element of pagan dualism from Greek philosophy. This pagan philosophy has crept into our thinking regarding work, faith, government, family, and community. Through the teachings of Augustine and other early Church fathers educated in Greek thought, this duality has seeped into the Church and displaced the teachings of the original authors of the Bible. In this regard, Nancy Pearcy warns, "The danger is that if Christians do not *consciously* develop a biblical approach to [worldview], then we will *un*consciously absorb some other philosophical approach."[7] The unconscious absorption of this pagan philosophy is a threat to leading an integral life, and it has led to the dissatisfaction and frustration of countless workers at their jobs and countless members of local churches around the world.

Pearcy details this subtle influence well, noting that in classical thought, beginning with Plato, there is a "stark dichotomy be-

---

7 Pearcey, Nancy. *Total Truth: Liberating Christianity from Its Cultural Captivity*. (Wheaton, IL: Crossway Books, 2008), 44.

tween matter and spirit, treating the material realm as though it were less valuable than the spiritual realm—and sometimes outright evil."[8] This reflects what she calls the Two-Story approach to reality, namely, an Upper Story (that is, thought, spirituality, a contemplative life) and a Lower Story (that is, the material world and its manual labor and affairs). The Two-Story philosophy uses Plato's word picture of a cave as the best-known analogy. Plato postulates that people are tantalized by the shadows they see on the cave wall, which he equates with the material world. They are not seeking the true forms at the mouth of the cave that are casting those shadows, and so, they have settled for the material world rather than aiming for the highest forms of spiritual and cognitive truth. As Plato's reasoning goes, those highest forms of Goodness, Truth, and Beauty await the philosopher who breaks free from the errors and illusions of the material world's cave. "It is the function of *education* to lead men out of the cave into the world of light."[9]

So, the Upper Story consists of Forms (Eternal Reason), and the Lower Story consists of Matter (Eternal Formless Flux).

This is so embedded into our way of thinking that I quote Pearcey here at length to address it,

> *But the Greeks defined the human dilemma as metaphysical—the problem is that we are physical, material beings. And if the material world is bad, then the goal of the religious life is to avoid, suppress, and ultimately escape from the material aspects of life. Manual labor was regarded as less valuable than prayer and meditation. Mar-*

---

8 Ibid., 74

9 Stumpf, Samuel Enoch. *Philosophy: History and Problems*. (London: McGraw-Hill Education, 1994), 53.

riage and sexuality were rejected in favor of celibacy. Ordinary social life was on a lower plane than life in hermitages and monasteries. The goal of spiritual life was to free the mind from the evil world of the body and the senses, so it could ascend to God.

Does this sound familiar? It describes much of the spirituality of the church fathers and the Middle Ages. The really committed Christian was the one who rejected ordinary work and family life, withdrawing to a monastery to live a life of prayer and contemplation. A Christian vocation was conceived of as separate from ordinary human life and community.

In the context of our discussion here, substituting missions demonstrates what is so often expressed in our thinking in the Church: "The *really* committed Christian is the one who rejects ordinary work and family life and serves God as a pastor or missionary." We teach with *When Everything Is Missions* and *What Is the Mission of the Church?* that everyday, ordinary people cannot accomplish the mission of the Church by doing everyday, ordinary things. Those everyday, ordinary things belong to the Lower Story. That is the activity of the material world to be escaped from. Rather, *really* committed Christians must abandon their ordinary work and devote themselves exclusively to evangelism, the thinking goes. That is true spirituality. That is missions. In truth, that is the Upper Story of Neo-Platonism.

The fact is, this philosophical dualism from Plato simply is not biblical. The Bible makes explicitly clear that matter has not existed for eternity, but God created it, and "*It was very good*" (Genesis 1:31). Since it was created by God, it reflected his character and nature, which are inherently good.

Regarding the notion that only "professional" Christians are really carrying out the mission of God's people, the writers of the Reformation seem antithetically opposed to this as well. The core of the Reformation was the doctrine of the priesthood of the believer,

> *But you are a chosen race, a royal priesthood, a holy nation, a people of his own, so that you may proclaim the virtues of the one who called you out of darkness into his marvelous light.*
>
> *1 Peter 2:9*

Lay believers were affirmed in approaching God directly without the intervention of an intermediary such as a priest or a monk or a nun to serve as a go-between. In other words, even laypeople could approach God and do God's work. Today's insistence that only "professional" missionaries or pastors are truly serving God emasculates the Church of its vast witness through everyday people and returns us to the errors of medieval Catholicism and its dependence on Greek thought.

Rather, the Reformers rejected this Two-Story Christianity and affirmed our participation in the created order of work and family. Consider the position of Martin Luther:

> *Whereas in the Middle Ages, the word vocation was used strictly of religious callings (priest, monk, or nun), Martin Luther deliberately chose the same term for the vocation of being a merchant, farmer, weaver, or homemaker. Running a business or a household was not the least bit inferior to being a priest or a nun, he argued, because all were ways of obeying the Cultural Mandate—of participating in God's work in maintaining and caring for His creation.*[10]

If you, then, are a believing farmer or a plumber or mechanic or electrician or barista or waitress who contributes through your work to society running smoothly, you will not find your work devalued in the message of this book. Your work has value, and we are all dependent on it even though it may not be "professional" Christian work. You are not a second-class citizen in the Kingdom living out second-class work. You did not somehow miss out on God's best for you.

Instead, you will find a message that affirms the integration of all of life for witness and service of the Creator rather than the Two-Story duality of sacred and secular that hamstrings your valuable contribution to society. The message you will find here is *the integral life*.

By reducing "mission" to only one sense of the word (that is, activities we are sent cross-culturally to accomplish) and further confining those activities to only speak of the mission of the Church, Stephen Neill and others have perpetuated the pagan dualism we inherited from Augustine, Chrysostom, and other early Church fathers similarly trained in Greek thought. This

---

10 Nancy Pearcey, *Total Truth: Liberating Christianity from Its Cultural Captivity* (Wheaton, IL: Crossway Books, 2008), 81.

reductionism is overly simplistic, and it does not encapsulate the Bible's thorough teaching on the value and goodness of Creation and the value and goodness of our work in fulfilling our cultural mandate, a term brought into use by Klaas Schilder to express "the original commandment by the Lord to our first parents, and thus to all humanity."[11]

To pull this section together, then, there is a difference between "mission" and "missions." In defining "mission," it is critical to recognize the many different missions of the Bible and their relation to one another. Accomplishing a mission (that is, goal, purpose, aim) entails the successful completion of many missions (that is, sending activities that support the mission). Finally, missions can serve a larger umbrella mission without the need to reduce them to the Two-Story dualism of Neo-Platonic thought.

---

11 Edgar, William. *Created and Creating: A Biblical Theology of Culture*. Downers Grove, IL: IVP Academic, 2016), 73.

The Telos Tower **Brick by Brick**

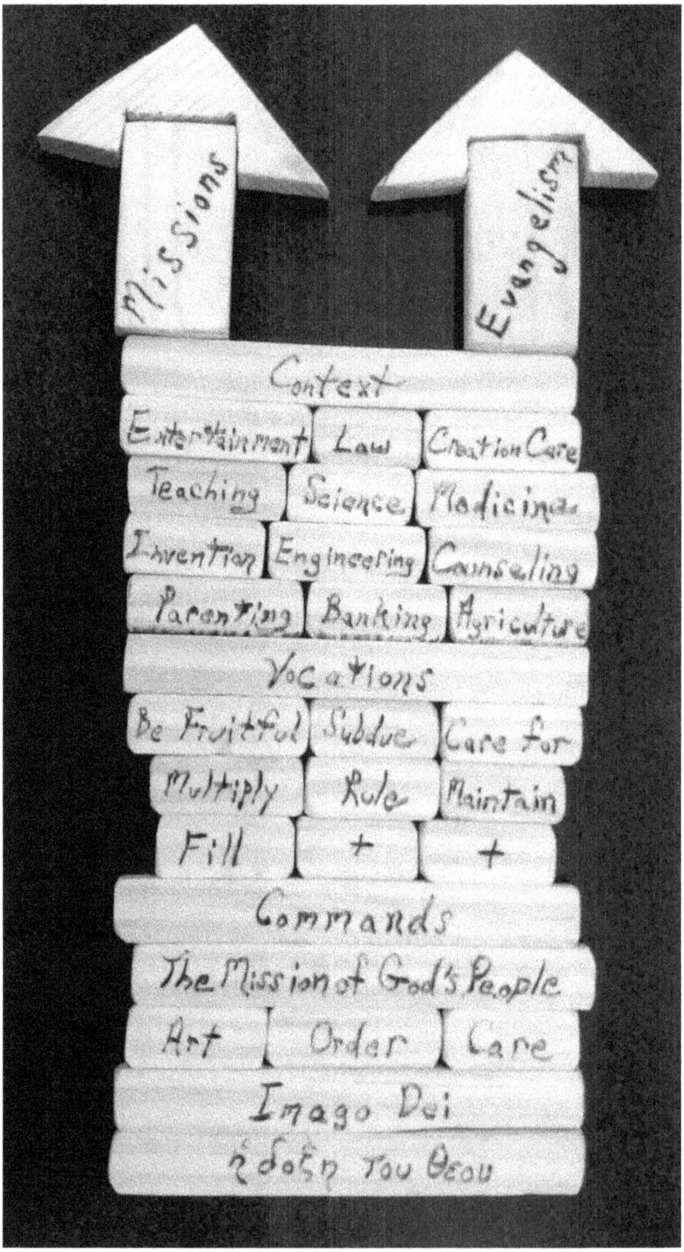

The Telos Tower from Scripture

As we turn our attention to the detail of the mission of people, it is important to note at this point that we are looking first at the mission of all people even before disobedience corrupted us with sinful intent. God created all humans to reflect his image. That being the case, what are the specific commands that God gives to people? These are obviously important because these are the true mission/purpose/aim of God's people that he first intended. These commands can be grouped into three broad areas:

Art (Creator)

- "Be fruitful."
- "Multiply."
- "Fill the earth."

Order (Curator)

- "Subdue."
- "Rule."

Care (Cultivator)

- "Care for."
- "Maintain."

In broad strokes, then, these are the things we were created to do. This is what we were made for. By doing these, we accomplish the mission of God's people. By doing these things, we express our created purpose. *God's image* is clearly seen through the actions of *art*, *order*, and *care*. When we do those actions, we show ourselves to be creators, curators, and cultivators, just as God is. When we do those actions, we reflect his image.

As God's summary of his own plan for people to reflect his image through art, order, and care, God himself proclaimed, "*It was very good!*" (Genesis 1:31). So, our activities as *creators*, *curators*, and *cultivators* reflect God's image. Let me state that again to make this point abundantly clear; our activities as *creators*, *curators*, and *cultivators* reflect God's image. We are made in the image of God, so we reflect these aspects of his nature. Even though our moral image was utterly corrupted by sin, our natural image reflects the nature of God irrespective of the sin that came through Adam and Eve.[12] At no point does the Bible say that we lost our natural ability to reflect God's image. We still bear his image in our very being. That being the case, our first mission as humankind is to bear the image of God for his glory.

Of course, the Fall of Adam and Eve dramatically affected all of humanity through moral corruption as well as through the curses God placed on man and woman. It even made "ordinary, everyday" activities much more difficult. The pain women experience in childbirth was greatly increased. Men continued to care for and maintain the earth, but it was only by the sweat of their brow. Nonetheless, these ordinary, everyday activities that people were given to do before the Fall continued after the Fall, and they continued to reflect God's image after the Fall as well.

It is worthwhile to look in detail, then, at just what those *Commands* are from before the Fall:

---

12 Charles F. Pfeiffer, Howard Frederic Vos, and John Rea, *The Wycliffe Bible Encyclopedia* (Chicago, IL: Moody Press, 1975), 832.

> *Then God said, "Let us make humankind in our image, after our likeness, so they may rule over the fish of the sea and the birds of the air, over the cattle, and over all the earth, and over all the creatures that move on the earth." God created humankind in his own image, in the image of God he created them, male and female he created them. God blessed them and said to them, "**Be fruitful** and **multiply**! **Fill** the earth and **subdue** it! **Rule** over the fish of the sea and the birds of the air and every creature that moves on the ground."*
>
> *Genesis 1:26–28*

So, man and woman were created with the express purpose of bearing the image and likeness of God. Part of that meant exercising dominion over all the created universe, but there are specific commands that are given to humans in order to live out that mandate. Specifically, those commands are to be fruitful, to multiply, to fill the earth, to subdue it, and to rule over every living thing. Additionally, we read a few verses later,

> *The Lord God took the man and placed him in the orchard in Eden to **care for** it and to **maintain** it.*
>
> *Genesis 2:15*

This caring for and maintaining the land serves as a governor over the commands to subdue and rule. For instance, our subduing and ruling might give us the right to burn fossil fuels indiscriminately, but if that means that we cause an acid rain catastrophe that destroys the habitat of one of the Great Lakes so that it is declared dead (Lake Erie in 1970), our dominion has transgressed our care and maintenance of the earth. The commands to care for and maintain prevent us from exploiting the earth and its resources to destruction.

So, these seven commands give us the means by which we actively exhibit the image and likeness of God. In doing them, we exhibit the art, order, and care that we see in the Creator God. Indeed, all moral actions we do even today in being fruitful, multiplying, filling the earth, subduing it, having dominion over it, working it, and caring for it exhibit the art, order, and care we see in the Creator God.

Of course, these general actions are lived out in our lives through our *Vocations*. These vocations can be any number of occupations, but there are a number of them highlighted in the Telos Tower to demonstrate how they fulfill the mandate we were given at Creation. By way of illustration, *Parents* exhibit fruitfulness in bringing forth children to fill all the earth. This act of creation of something where there was previously nothing exhibits the nature of *art* or creation that we see in God himself.

Likewise, an *Inventor* creates something useful and elegant where there was nothing before. I'm grateful for the inventors who exhibited the image of God through the fruitfulness of creating a Bluetooth keyboard for me to write this book.

Those producing moral *Entertainment* exhibit the creative nature of God built into them by giving us something beautiful to listen to, see, watch, or experience.

Those in *Teaching* professions are involved in the creation and dissemination of knowledge. The chemistry teacher has students plan the combination of two solvents and the hypothesized effect. Then, the students create knowledge by experiencing the effect of the combination.

So, our fruitfulness, multiplying, and filling of the earth reflects God's image of Art and fulfills our mandate to create. In a similar manner, we are commanded to subdue the earth and to have dominion over it. These commands demonstrate the order that God himself brought to Creation. At one time, the heavenly bodies consisted of primordial slough before they were brought together into orderly stars, planets, and moons. God graciously gave us the regularity of planetary motion to bring order to something that was previously disordered. Indeed, he brought further order to the earth itself by separating the waters and making the sky and by gathering the waters together to reveal dry ground beneath this water world. These clear delineations and boundaries bring order to an otherwise disordered world.

We reflect the orderly nature of God when we bring order out of disorder. When we subdue the earth through *Science*, for example, we bring classifications and order to all of Creation, just as Adam was instructed to do specifically by naming the animals. We bring order and demonstrate our dominion over Creation through occupations like *Banking* or *Engineering*. The banker looks at resources and creates products like mortgages and loans that allow those resources to benefit more and more people for businesses to be created or homes to be built. Engineers see the possibility of resources, say, across a river, and they think, *If we build a bridge, we can bring those resources under our dominion or use.* Even *Lawyers* and attorneys and judges reflect the orderly nature of the image of God when they uphold the orderly boundaries of what is lawful and what is not. These occupations and many others demonstrate the nature of order within us from the Creator himself.

All of that being said, this Art and Order is not unrestrained, but it is governed by the injunctions "*to care for it and to maintain it.*" We are given responsibility for the welfare of the plants and animals of the Garden of Eden and, by implication, all of the universe under our dominion.

Specifically in this regard, one of the most common occupations through the millennia has been *Agriculture,* where we employ ourselves with the welfare of plants and animals. Additionally, those involved in *Medicine* or dentistry care for people by providing the best environment for them to grow and flourish. *Counselors* and pastors do something similar by providing for people's spiritual and emotional well-being. Even those directly involved in *Creation Care,* such as forest rangers, firefighters, or those working in the Environmental Protection Agency, reflect the image of God through their work in caring for and maintaining Creation.

All of this provides the *Context* for our witness. It is critical to reaffirm that the mission of God's people must include *Missions* and *Evangelism.* Sharing the Good News of Jesus is the pinnacle of the narrative of the Bible, so we cannot simply go about our daily lives and neglect sharing the Gospel. The point of this is that *our witness is not at odds with normal, everyday life; our normal lives reflect the image of God.* When we do this with special care and intent, we establish a context from which we can speak the truth of the Gospel.

In short, our work ethic reflects our faith epic. When people see the various acts of care and mercy, such as our care for "*orphans and widows in their adversity*" (James 1:27), they should recognize something out of the ordinary in that care. When we, as followers of Christ, model justice and righteousness because of our image of God, we show his Order and we establish context so that a world apart from God can see what it is like to be with God. When people see the integrity and honor of an accountant who does her fund reconciliations "*to the Lord and not for people*" (Colossians 3:23), she can share that her reason for that high integrity is found in Jesus. When a parent corrects a child and demonstrates the way that is right, he has built a platform with his work as a parent to speak about his ultimate purpose to reflect the image and likeness of God.

In this very tangible manner, our work ethic becomes the context from which we do evangelism and missions. The words of our evangelism and missions have meaning because they are couched in the context of the work we do as the people of God. *Our work ethic reflects our faith epic.*

Of First Importance

Despite this strong focus on the intrinsic value of our work and its part of our faith story, this does not diminish our need to share the Gospel. In order to dispel any notion of this, consider two quotations from the writings of Paul to clarify the absolute necessity of sharing the Gospel:

> *For I passed on to you as of first importance what I also received—that Christ died for our sins according to the scriptures, and that he was buried, and that he was raised on the third day according to the scriptures, and that he appeared to Cephas, then to the twelve.*
>
> 1 Corinthians 15:3

From this, it is clear that whatever God's mission is for his people, the preaching of the Gospel is the first and foremost aim of the Church. Being members of the Church, then, the preaching of the Gospel is our chief aim.

Secondly, with the Gospel being of first importance, the significance of specifically calling people to decision about the Gospel cannot be left to chance or implicit activity. The Gospel must be explicitly shared with all people everywhere. This point is driven home by Matt Chandler in his book *The Explicit Gospel*, "You hanging out having a beer with your buddy so he can see that Christians are cool is not what we're called to do. You're eventually going to have to open up your mouth and share the gospel. When the pure gospel is shared, people respond."[13]

The Apostle Paul comes to this same conclusion no less forcefully,

> *How are they to call on one they have not believed in? And how are they to believe in one they have not heard of? And how are they to hear without someone preaching to them?*
>
> *Romans 10:14*

In order to have "*an enormous crowd that no one could count, made up of persons from every nation, tribe, people, and language*" (Revelation 7:9), each of you needs to "*confess with your mouth that Jesus is Lord and believe in your heart that God raised him from the dead*" (Romans 10:9). This is without debate.

So, it is imperative to affirm that the mission of God's people is *no less than* missions, that is, sending people cross-culturally to share the Gospel.

On the other hand, when we look at the totality of the Bible, what shows the character of God that we should model? How is the God of the Bible different from other gods? How does the character of God affect the mission of God's people?

---

13 Matt Chandler and Jared Wilson, *The Explicit Gospel* (Wheaton, IL: Crossway Books, 2014), 81.

CHAPTER 3–CREATORS

#WeCreateBecauseHeCreated

The creation of the telegraph recounted earlier exemplified that there is always more culture to be added to culture. As we explore deeper into the ways that we reflect the character and nature of God, it is important to note that there is always more culture to be made to make something even more useful of the world.

Defining culture as "what we make of the world" is a simple and elegant definition that Andy Crouch attributes to Ken Myers.[14] In expounding on this definition, however, Crouch is careful to point out that it is not merely a matter of "what we make of the world" because none of us starts with a cultural blank slate. In his words, "There is a paradox here, however. Because culture is cumulative—because every cultural good builds on and incorporates elements of culture that have come before—cultural creativity never starts from scratch. Culture is what we make of the world—we start not with a blank slate but with all the richly encultured world that previous generations have handed to us."[15]

None of us starts from ground zero with no culture whatsoever. None of us lives in a cultural vacuum. None of us lives devoid of culture. Rather, we are all given raw materials and culture that have been passed down to us, and it is from those raw materials

---

14 Andy Crouch, *Culture Making: Recovering Our Creative Calling* (Downers Grove, IL: Intervarsity Press, 2013), 99.
15 Ibid.

and culture that have been entrusted to us that we make something of the world. In effect, then, we take culture that is given to us and make more culture. In our role as Creators, we are culture makers.

In this discussion of creating or making culture, we would be remiss if we did not highlight that culture itself is tied to an environment of growth and flourishing. This sense of culture can be related, for example, to the culture of a Petri dish. Julius Richard Petri created the small, cylindrical dish used to culture or grow bacteria. He created an environment that was conducive to growth so that he could further study those bacteria. In a similar manner, culture both creates an environment conducive to growth and describes the innovations themselves that create that culture.

This environment that is conducive to growth is something we will explore in a future chapter, but at this point, this environment conducive to growth is tied directly to our ability to make creations that are conducive to that growth. In other words, our role as creators is tied to our role as culture makers.

To illustrate this integral link, consider the first cultural product in all of Creation. Genesis 1 recounts the story of Creation and finishes with the culmination of God creating man and woman in his own likeness on the sixth day. Keep in mind that the chapter divisions we have in our Bibles were added millennia after the events of this story, so it is important not to make too much of the division between Genesis 1 and Genesis 2. That being the case, the story of Genesis 2 continues,

> *The heavens and the earth were completed with everything that was in them. By the seventh day God finished the work that he had been doing,*

> *and he ceased on the seventh day all the work that he had been doing. God blessed the seventh day and made it holy because on it he ceased all the work that he had been doing in creation.*
>
> *Genesis 2:1–3*

The first element of culture that was given to humans is the Sabbath, a day of rest. Of course, language is replete with culture and inseparable from culture, but the language that is used to communicate with humans is treated as an assumption rather than a cultural good that is endowed on humankind by the Creator. That being the case, the Sabbath as a day of rest is the first artifact of culture and serves as the predecessor to all culture that follows.

When God instituted a day of rest for all humankind, it was the creation of a cultural good that set one day apart from others. To be sure, every solar day is essentially the same. There is no banner across the sky that indicates today is Tuesday. The sun does not shine in a different color on Wednesday than it does on Saturday, so there was no external indicator that differentiated one day from another. Even so, God graciously gave the cultural good of the Sabbath to permit us a day of rest and so bring order to each week to mark our days. Not only this, but God instituted the Sabbath, knowing well the limitations of our finite bodies. He knew we would need rest, so he gave us a day of rest as the most conducive manner of growth. The Sabbath, as the simple institution of the first cultural good, then, shows God's creation of culture, his sense of order for our benefit, and his care for our growth. From the very first cultural good, God revealed his own nature of art, order, and care.

As another clear example, we can look at God's next cultural good, namely, a garden. When God himself planted a garden, it was not just to show that gardening was a good family-budgeting principle. The garden was a cultural good that had never been created before God created it. The garden delineated an intentional area of growth as distinct from the wild, untamed wilderness. It brought order to one particular area where there was otherwise disorder. Furthermore, the garden provided the most conducive environment for growth where man and woman had all they needed to thrive. Whereas the Sabbath was the first cultural good, the second cultural good was the creation of a garden that brought order to what was otherwise disordered, and it was the means of providing an environment most conducive to growth. The garden revealed God's own nature of art, order, and care.

When we approach the responsibility of the creation mandate/cultural mandate, we model the image and likeness of God in the very actions of fulfilling Genesis 1 and 2.

The Culture of Education

The creation we see in these chapters is not limited to mere cultural development. Indeed, the most obvious sense of being fruitful, multiplying, and filling the earth is the same sense that the fish of the sea and the birds of the air were given, namely, to produce offspring. For humans, however, the fruitfulness of producing offspring carries a purpose that no other creature has. When people produce offspring, they fill the earth with the image and likeness of God. Of course, this is by the Lord's created design, as we can see in the next commands to subdue the earth and to rule over it. We manifest God's rule of the earth by bearing his likeness across the whole of creation. "Humans were created to be God's deputies exercising dominion over creation."[16]

16 Nancy Pearcey, *Total Truth: Liberating Christianity from Its Cultural Captivity* (Wheaton, IL: Crossway Books, 2008), 159.

We have, then, two means of created design to be fruitful, multiply, and fill the earth. Most obviously, we are to reproduce and fill the earth with "God's deputies exercising dominion over creation." Secondly, we send those children forth full of innumerable innovations and cultural goods and creations and disciplines and inventions and wisdom that we have passed on to them. This, then, becomes the basis of education. Of note, education is not rooted in the dictates of cultural goods that governments desire for children in order to meet the needs of the state. Education is rooted in the image of God that is passed on to children to enable them to best fulfill their created design.

So, then, there are both the biological aspects of being fruitful, multiplying, and filling the earth, and there are the innovative aspects of being fruitful, multiplying, and filling the earth.

Creating Living Poetry

Before even addressing the specifics of the Creation story from Genesis, consider these words from the Apostle Paul, which show the reverence he had for God's creative work of creating people. As a first point of consideration, it must be noted that God's act of creation is no mere fabrication of a high school welding project. Rather, his very nature is poetically illustrated through the creation of people.

A well-known confessional passage of faith is Ephesians 2:8–10, which centers on the creation of humankind by concluding, "*For we are his creative work, having been created in Christ Jesus for good works that God prepared beforehand so we can do them.*" In English, it sounds like "creative work" or "workmanship" could be used to describe a high school welding project. A teacher might comment in the grading process, "Clean welds, no gaps, strong binding. All in all, good workmanship."

On the other hand, the original word used by Paul is much more colorful, and it doesn't take an expert in Koine Greek to appreciate Paul's word choice. A literal translation could be, "*For we are His poem, created in Christ Jesus.*" We are the result of artful, skillful craft. We are a decorative work of beauty and incredible design. When we affirm that we are God's creation, we affirm the character of the masterful Creator himself.

By way of contrast, the Bible does not say that parrots are made in the image of God. The Bible does not say that whales are made in the image of God. The Bible does not even say that chimpanzees or other primates are made in the image of God, but it does say that about humans. It says that we are created in God's image and likeness, that we are his poetic creation.

Our creation in the image and likeness of God is such an important feature of our nature and who we are that it is worth digging deeper to discover just how we model the image and likeness of God.

Being created in the image and likeness of God means that we are to look at what God has done *and do likewise*. As noted earlier, our fruitfulness does not just allow us to physically fill the earth. We use our fruitfulness to create new forms of art and new expressions of beauty, just as God did in creating us as his poem or workmanship. Reflecting the image of our beautiful Maker, we imitate his beauty in paintings, sculptures, photography, music, architecture, technology, delicacies of taste, and intoxicating scents. Our thirst for beauty is insatiable, just as our hunger for adventure is insatiable. We have these deep longings for beauty and aesthetic design because they reflect our Maker's expression of beauty and aesthetic design that we see manifest throughout the universe. From the laws of gravity that govern neutron stars to the breathtaking vistas of the Grand Canyon, we long to create like the Creator has created.

Summary

God himself is more than the "mere" Creator of all things. Creating all things as beautiful and elegantly complex as they are is not enough. Rather, God is also the first culture maker. When he gave humans the commands to "*Be fruitful and multiply! Fill the earth*," it was not merely biological as the command was given to the other parts of creation. God created us to be creators biologically in reproducing, physically in going to all the earth, and through beautiful innovations that reflect his image and likeness. In short, we create because he created.

CHAPTER 4—CURATORS

#OrderByDesign

Extreme Adventure

My doctor runs marathons. I suppose it is good for a doctor to practice what he preaches, but, to an outside observer, it would seem that Dr. Keith Moore is obsessed with marathons. To say that he merely runs marathons is an understatement.

A few years ago, he had this wild idea of running a marathon in each state. So, his marathon achievement is not just to run twenty-six point two miles. His marathon achievement is to run twenty-six point two miles fifty times.

Dr. Moore has only two marathons remaining, and as of this writing, he is scheduled to complete them in the next few weeks. He has noted that the travel itself can be more difficult than the marathon. He would often fly out Saturday evening, run a marathon Sunday morning, and fly home Sunday afternoon so he could be back to work on Monday. On one of his recent trips, he ran three marathons in three days. He didn't want to make three separate trips to North Dakota, South Dakota, and Wyoming, so he buzzed through them in three consecutive days.

In one sense, Dr. Moore is subduing the marathon race itself. Only one in 200 people in the United States ever complete even one marathon. On the other hand, Dr. Moore is dominating all of the United States. He is overcoming a massive challenge in *every* state and thereby subduing that challenge in the entire country. Congratulations, Dr. Moore!

Not to take anything from the monumental accomplishment of Dr. Moore, another notable person has conquered a monument itself. Usually, running a marathon is not considered a life-threatening endeavor, even though the first marathon run was fatal for its only participant. By contrast, free solo rock climbing is *always life-threatening*. In subduing free solo rock climbing, Alex Honnold is a freak of nature.

To understand the mortal danger Alex Honnold puts himself in, a list of types of rock climbing might be helpful. There are varying degrees of rock climbing, from basic mountaineering, when a person is hiking up a well-trodden trail, to scrambling, where hands and feet are used, to technical rock climbing, where the ascent is near vertical. Within the world of technical rock climbing, one can free climb, which means you are using ropes, harnesses, and anchors into the rock face for safety, but your ascent is unaided by these safety measures. Then, there is free solo climbing which uses no safety ropes, harnesses, or anchors whatsoever. A single mistake runs the risk of death.

Alex Honnold is an expert free solo climber. In fact, he envisioned a free solo climb of one of the most difficult mountain faces in the world, namely, El Capitan of Yosemite National Park in California. As recently as 1958, El Capitan was considered unclimbable whether using ropes or whatever support was available. Fifty-eight years later, Alex Honnold thought differently and even thought of climbing the massive 3200-foot face free solo.

The following year consisted of intensive training and memorization of specific holds, routes, and maneuvers. His specialized training for this climb included free climbing El Capitan forty to fifty times with safety equipment in preparation.

On June 3, 2017, Alex Honnold quietly left his camp with only a chalk bag strapped to his waist to keep his hands dry for grip. He made his free solo ascent of El Capitan without great fanfare but culminating in exhilarating dominance… of a mountain. Alex Honnold subdued a mountain under his will in a way that he is the only human ever to have done so.

Sadly, Alex calls himself a "born-again atheist" and does not have faith in God. Nonetheless, he cannot hide the image of God that is in his nature that reflects a deep urge in our very being to explore and overcome every obstacle. Regarding the risk he puts himself in, he says, "Look, I don't want to fall off and die either. But there is a satisfaction to challenging yourself and doing something well. That feeling is heightened when you are for sure facing death. You can't make a mistake."[17]

Our initiative and drive to overcome these obstacles are insatiable. Give us a 3200-foot rock face, give us the coldest continent, the largest wave, the deepest ocean, the driest, hottest desert, and we go there. That act of going is not merely one and done, but we use our innovation and ingenuity to create means to live there in those places, victorious over all the elements and challenges thrown our way.

We were made with the created design to rule the earth and to subdue it. There is no part of this earth that is beyond our dominion. Whether empire-commissioned explorers, government-contracted surveyors, or indomitable adventurers, we go into wild places and bring them under our order and dominion.

In the same way that God commissioned us to go into all the earth to be fruitful and multiply, God commissioned us to bring

---

17 Vasarhelyi, Elizabeth Chai, and Jimmy Chin. 2018. Free Solo. United States: National Geographic Documentary Films.

order from disorder. We go into wild, untamed places, but we do not leave them in that chaotic, disordered state. Rather, as God brought order from disorder, we bring order from disorder.

This point is shared succinctly by Andy Crouch: "Genesis 1 is a sequence of acts of ordering, as the Creator gradually carves out a habitable environment. The first chapter of Genesis records a series of divisions—order from chaos, light from darkness, heaven from earth, sea from land—each of which makes the world more amenable for the flourishing of creativity." He continues with this summary, "So, in a way, the Creator's greatest gift to his creation is the gift of structure—not a structure which locks the world, let alone the Creator himself, into eternal mechanical repetition, but a structure which provides freedom. And those who are made in his image will also be both creators and rulers."[18]

Consider, for example, time itself. Time is a gift of grace from the Creator. In its most basic definition, time is the sequential ordering of events. By this measurement, there are events that have happened (past), events that are happening (present), and events that will happen (future). God, in his mercy, graciously put planets and stars into motion by which we might measure time in even more detail. This further ordered our lives so that we have nighttime and daytime. With the motion of the Moon, we recognize months. With the division of the Earth's rotation around the sun, we know solar days and years.

Even our simplest sense of time being past, present, and future is something the rest of the animal kingdom does not have. Yet, our concept of time is far more replete with the sense of millennia, centuries, decades, years, months, weeks, days, hours, min-

---

18 Andy Crouch, *Culture Making: Recovering Our Creative Calling* (Downers Grove, IL: Intervarsity Press, 2013), 21-22.

utes, seconds, nanoseconds, picoseconds, etc. As noted earlier, our sense of time shows an extreme inclination to the ordering of events. In short, we cannot help but order our world because of the image of God we bear in our nature.

Time is an example of the unquenchable thirst for order that we have in our nature, but there are many other examples. Every road that we build through a desert, a forest, a plain, a city, a mountain, or over a river shows this orderly nature and dominion. Every scientific endeavor is an attempt to understand the natural working of things, and it is an exhibition of the desire to order the universe.

The U.S. military built the Global Positioning System (GPS) to be able to identify the location of an individual or a target or a ship or a bomb in an instant. The civilian version of GPS can identify the location of a phone, for example, to a single meter anywhere on the Earth's surface, which is especially helpful for those of us who have misplaced it somewhere in the house, but we're not sure where. Google took the innovation of GPS and improved on it by overlaying that one-meter location onto publicly available maps that we use for navigation in cars, on bikes, or on hikes. Another company, what3words, recognized that there is a need to communicate a specific location, not just a street address, so they improved on Google's mapping system to divide the entire surface of the Earth into 3-meter by 3-meter squares. In fact, the engineers have labeled 57 trillion of these squares to cover the whole Earth. With three-word combinations, you can identify the exact square to share the 3-meter by 3-meter square of your position. For example, the coffee shop where I have written much of this book is ///clan.maxim.assure. If I want to meet my friend at that specific coffee shop, I can direct him to w3w.co/clan.maxim.assure. *What3words* is an example of order upon order upon order. Our thirst for order knows no bounds.

Whether those boxes and grids are temporal or spatial, or even legal, we exhibit order. That legal order is manifested as well through unbelievers such as the Law Code of Hammurabi or followers of God such as Moses. They all manifest our nature and our leaning toward defining orderly boxes of what is acceptable or not acceptable. Of course, our own Supreme Court of the US has shown through decisions like Dred Scott v. Sanford or Roe v. Wade that sin corrupts even the minds of justices, and they have made grievous, sinful errors. Notwithstanding, moral attorneys, lawyers, judges, and justices reflect the image of God in their desire for legal order.

Summary

"Be fruitful and multiply! Fill the earth and subdue it! Rule over the fish of the sea and the birds of the air and every creature that moves on the ground." These words of Genesis 1:28 set the course for our insatiable thirst for adventure and order and dominion. Where we bring order from disorder, we display that we are made in the image of God. We put on display this characteristic of God himself that he commanded us to exhibit throughout the whole world. In short, we fulfill our role as curators, bringing order where before there was chaos.

CHAPTER 5–CULTIVATORS

#CareForGrowth

Finally, God provided all that is needed to survive and thrive on earth. Indeed, in the retelling of the Creation story with deeper detail in Genesis 2, God himself planted a garden. He did not merely drop humans into a desert or the Antarctic or into a thicket in the wilderness, wishing them the best of luck. He expressed care for us by providing all we needed to eat and be healthy and flourish and grow. As a matter of fact, God himself visited the first humans to check on their growth, health, and well-being. He managed the growth, or culture, of his Creation, and when we cultivate growth, we reflect his image and likeness. Indeed, the culture we ourselves exhibit manifests the growth we see in all civilization. God is a Cultivator. Like God, we are *cultivators.*

"The Lord God planted an orchard." This statement alone would have set the Jewish religion apart from virtually all religions of the ancient world. Revisiting Plato again, the Two-Story philosophical approach he engendered rested on the duality that matter and all that is part of the material world is, at best, a negative diversion from the world of the true forms of what is spiritual, virtuous, and filled with contemplative thought. For the Hebrew God to get his hands dirty in earthly soil and plant an orchard, well, this would have been just too much for the Greeks to wrap their minds around. On the other hand, it is fundamental to the Hebrew faith.

God created all matter and coalesced that matter into rich, vibrant soil with all the nutrients and bacteria for plants and trees to produce rich, healthful, and delicious fruit. Indeed, when God planted a garden, we can understand that he put the plants and trees into the soil. He did not declare this as dirty or second-rate. God declared this was good.

Building on this act of Art or creation, our subsequent work as creators necessarily entails cultivation of the goods we are entrusted with. Crouch writes, "*creation begins with cultivation*—taking care of the good things that culture has already handed on to us. The first responsibility of culture makers is not to make something new but to become fluent in the cultural tradition to which we are responsible. Before we can be culture makers, we must be culture keepers."[19] The two roles are intertwined. They support one another, and together, they form an integral whole.

The Hebrew account of Genesis 2 is devoid of any mention of deep, philosophical reasoning being more virtuous for God than simply getting his "hands" into the soil. Rather, the account is as simple as "*the Lord God planted an orchard.*" This was physical, manual labor. Even the word "manual" indicates it is labor by hand, not in some distant, removed, automated manner. The result of this was an ordered, productive garden that provided all that humans would need to survive and thrive. The Two-Story approach falls on its face just like the Philistine god Dagon.[20]

Whereas the Greeks presented the material world as bad in a clear duality, the Bible presents the material world as originally good. Since the material world was created by God, it reflects the character and nature of God, which is inherently good.

---

19 Andy Crouch, *Culture Making: Recovering Our Creative Calling* (Downers Grove, IL: Intervarsity Press, 2013), 101.
20 1 Samuel 5.4.

The Grove and the Forest

By the end of high school, most students have a vocabulary of around 20,000 words. That number is astounding itself, but for me, it was in high school that I learned the difference between a grove and a forest. President Franklin Roosevelt was famous for employing massive numbers of job-seekers during the Great Depression, planting enormous groves of pine trees throughout the northern Midwest. For some reason, when I was a child and I would ride past these groves with my family, I thought it was simply a mysterious fluke of nature that this type of tree dropped its seeds in perfect rows for miles on end. It never crossed my mind that thousands of men and women were employed to plant every one of those trees by hand.

Contrast those massive groves with other massive forests throughout Wisconsin. These forests tangle wildly upward with all sorts of underbrush fighting to catch the glimmers of light that might break through the canopy of large oaks mixed in with maple trees and pine trees and elms and hickory, and so on. The underbrush is nearly impassable with thorns and thickets that give a very real sense of the curse God put on the land after Adam's Fall. In short, forests grow wildly in whatever chaotic manner nature would have it. They are inhospitable and largely unproductive in their supply of food or shelter or resources for people.

When we consider the simple act of God planting a garden, we recognize this as a gracious gift and act of care. As noted, the Lord could have created humans and set them free in a forest or a desert or a salt flat or a rugged mountain range or an ice-capped glacier. In any of these places, God would have completed his creative work, but we could describe his choice of placement as desertion of the first humans. It would have expressed apathy toward our welfare and even cruelty as every fear would be triggered by the unprotected environment we were placed in. In short, it would have resembled the heinous practice of *exposito* described at length by O.M. Bakke.[21] Defenseless infants were simply placed outside in a deserted place to die. Adam and Eve would have been no less defenseless than infants in any of those hostile environments triggering every fear the amygdala could produce.

Conversely, note what God actually did in expressing his image of care and nurture. He placed Adam and Eve in a garden that he planted with select fruit and vegetables to ensure that they had everything for protection and provision. This was an act of love and care that fostered growth (that is, culture). Put another way, "One who cultivates tries to create the most fertile conditions for good things to survive and thrive."[22] We have the sense that the Garden of Eden was a place of peace that triggered emotions of gratitude and care through the prefrontal cortex, not one of fear and anxiety driven by the amygdala.

In speaking of care and maintenance, it is helpful to define what they are, specifically in respect to Creation. Before defining what care is, we can easily identify what it is not. Instinctively, we know that neglect, abandonment, and exploitation do not express care. They express self-centeredness by taking or withholding something of value from those who need it.

On the other hand, care is centered entirely on others. The care of a shepherd, for instance, is focused on the welfare of the sheep, whether that means protecting them from wolves or protecting them from self-harm such as falls. At the same time, the shepherd also provides them with shelter, food, drink,

21 Odd Magne Bakke, *When Children Became People: The Birth of Childhood in Early Christianity* (Minneapolis, MN: Fortress Press, 2007), chapter 4.
22 Andy Crouch, *Culture Making: Recovering Our Creative Calling* (Downers Grove, IL: Intervarsity Press, 2013), 103.

and comfort. Care is providing all that is necessary for growth, whether for sheep, in our example, or other examples such as crops of wheat or tomatoes or children or citizens.

Maintenance is keeping things running smoothly in the way they were intended. If you fail to maintain your car by not adding oil, the vehicle will no longer operate in the way it was intended. Failing to plant cover crops to prevent erosion will result in a field with no topsoil that is no longer useful for agriculture.

So, we see by the example of God's image that we are to express care and maintenance of Creation through our image-bearing. As a basis for that care and maintenance, we must first recognize our own role as stewards of all God has given us. Adam and Eve could make no claim to ownership of the Garden of Eden or of earth itself. Subsequently, none of their descendants could make that claim, so it is important to recognize that all we have is a gift. This is a posture of dependence on God, and it is a posture of simplicity.

Richard Foster summarizes this principle, "Simplicity means a return to the posture of dependence. Like children, we live in a spirit of trust. What we have we receive as a gift."[23] This recognition guards us from a posture of pride and arrogance regarding possessions and even earth itself. It places us in a posture of looking after the interests and well-being of what has been entrusted to us.

This is evident in the biblical example of Abraham, in the Law of Moses regarding property, in the teaching of Jesus through parables, in the care of widows and orphans in the Epistle of James, in the protection of the Creation in the Revelation of John and in myriad other places where mercy for others trumps our own individual rights.

---

23 Richard J. Foster, *Freedom of Simplicity: Revised Edition: Finding Harmony in a Complex World* (New York, NY: HarperOne, 2010), 19.

Of First Importance – Reprise

As an example to this effect, consider Abraham's promise from God:

> *Now the Lord said to Abram, "Go out from your country, your relatives, and your father's household to the land that I will show you. Then I will make you into a great nation, and I will bless you, and I will make your name great, so that you will exemplify divine blessing. I will bless those who bless you, but the one who treats you lightly I must curse, so that all the families of the earth may receive blessing through you."*
>
> *Genesis 12:1*

In the example of Abraham, we have a link between the land that he was given by the Lord and the prosperity he would experience in becoming a great nation. Indeed, through this great nation, all nations would be blessed. Nevertheless, the land is Abraham's means of achieving and maintaining his prosperity that would be a blessing to all of his descendants, and ultimately, to all nations.

To be sure, the chief blessing given to all nations is Jesus as the redeeming Messiah, just as the Apostle Paul concludes in 1 Corinthians 15:3–8:

> *For I passed on to you as of first importance what I also received—that Christ died for our sins according to the scriptures, and that he was buried, and that he was raised on the third day according*

> *to the scriptures, and that he appeared to Cephas, then to the twelve. Then he appeared to more than 500 of the brothers and sisters at one time, most of whom are still alive, though some have fallen asleep. Then he appeared to James, then to all the apostles. Last of all, as though to one born at the wrong time, he appeared to me also.*

Jesus as the King of the Universe is of utmost importance. However, there are other blessings that came to the nations through the descendants of Abraham. Again, Paul notes, "… *First of all, the Jews were entrusted with the oracles of God*" (Romans 3:2). Of course, this included God's ceremonial and moral laws given through Moses. Through those same laws, God gave the principle of rest through the Sabbath, dignity and personhood to those bearing the image of God, standards of justice and equity for land rights and property, release of slaves, and return of property during the Year of Jubilee, mercy and care for those in need, and so on.

A Land Flowing with Milk and Honey

Consider the equitable distribution of land made among the descendants of Abraham and what that meant to the people. Land was the means of providing for one's family. Possession of land meant gainful employment. For those who were so destitute that they had to sell their lands and even enslave themselves or their family members, all was to be restored to its original equitable state every fifty years during the Year of Jubilee. This ensured God's original intention that no family should be deprived of the basic right to provide for themselves. That being said, we have no record of the Israelites obeying God in this or ever keeping the Year of Jubilee, but the law was nonetheless given to prevent hoarding of real estate.

Richard Foster writes again,

> *"This principle of equitable distribution rather than hoarding, and managership rather than ownership, was as revolutionary then as it is now. What would happen if this idea—that the purpose of the land is to serve the needs of humanity rather than provide the means of self-aggrandizement—were to be accepted today? What would that say to our real estate investments? Perhaps such an approach would not meet with general approval, but what if Christians were to believe that the land was for the good of all people alike? Is it possible that this group alone could unleash resources that would amputate starvation from the face of the earth?"*[24]

This is the level of care that was in the original intent of God's ceremonial and moral law. God did not intend conditions for the rich to grow richer and the poor to grow poorer. Israel was to model this equity to all nations.

Care, Mercy, and Justice

The people of God, then, were set apart with certain commands to be an example for all nations. They were not to be the sort of people who simply sponged up wealth for their own consumption with boats. For instance, Chris Janson sings a song called

24 Richard J. Foster, *Freedom of Simplicity: Revised Edition: Finding Harmony in a Complex World* (New York, NY: HarperOne, 2010), 25.

"Buy Me a Boat," where he says, "Money can't buy happiness, but it could buy me a boat." The people of God were supposed to set themselves apart from this sort of thinking. Several of those commands that set them apart were being a blessing to all nations (Genesis 12), demonstrating justice and righteousness in a corrupt world (Genesis 18), exhibiting humility and mercy (Micah 6), setting captives free (Isaiah 61, Luke 7), caring for widows and orphans (James 1), and even exhibiting an excellent work ethic (Matthew 5, Colossians 3). Let's look at a few of these in more detail.

Throughout Scripture, we often see justice paired with righteousness. That being said, they are not identical. The meanings are certainly intertwined and influence one another, but they are not the same from a Hebrew perspective.

Justice is a fiduciary term, whereas righteousness is a moral and ethical term. Justice is the idea of "rendering to others what is their due [and] lies close to the idea of fairness. This is a term employed to describe justice in economics, the exchange of goods according to an equivalent value, and the distribution of goods according to need and merit."[25]

As such, taking advantage of the plight of the poor or widows or orphans or resident aliens is clear injustice. As an example of this sort of injustice, consider the words of Amos, a farmer, prophet, and author of the Bible,

> *The Israelites hate anyone who arbitrates at the city gate; they despise anyone who speaks honestly.*

---

25 Charles F. Pfeiffer, Howard Frederic Vos, and John Rea, *The Wycliffe Bible Encyclopedia* (Chicago, IL: Moody Press, 1975), 980.

Therefore, because you make the poor pay taxes on their crops and exact a grain tax from them, you will not live in the houses you built with chiseled stone, nor will you drink the wine from the fine vineyards you planted. Certainly I am aware of your many rebellious acts and your numerous sins. You torment the innocent, you take bribes, and you deny justice to the needy at the city gate. For this reason whoever is smart keeps quiet in such a time, for it is an evil time. Seek good and not evil so you can live!

Then the Lord God of Heaven's Armies just might be with you, as you claim he is. Hate what is wrong, love what is right. Promote justice at the city gate. Maybe the Lord God of Heaven's Armies will have mercy on those who are left from Joseph.

Amos 5:10–15

The village gate itself was thought of as the "courthouse" where grievances were heard and decisions were made to establish equitable distribution of wealth. In this case, the Israelites were under divine judgment because they did not uphold the cause of the poor in their decisions. The rich assumed that since they had real estate with strong homes built of hewn stone and plentiful vineyards, they did not need to give regard to the Lord's injunctions for justice toward the poor. As recompense for their injustice, the very thing they were relying on, namely, their land as their source of income, would be stripped from them. Their only hope was to establish justice at the gate.

On the other hand, righteousness carried the sense of an action or decision being in line with God's ordinances. Moral failings such as adultery or murder or dishonoring father and mother certainly fell short of God's ordinances, so they made a person unrighteous. On top of that, the moral failing of injustice, such as an unjust decision at the gates in favor of the rich exploiting the poor, also made a person unrighteous.

Of course, defrauding someone of possessions was a serious matter in itself, with restitution necessary (e.g., Exodus 21–22). However, defrauding someone of the ability to earn a living (that is, taking land) was especially grievous, which is why widows and orphans were in the plight they were. In short, they had no claim to land inheritance, so they had no means of earning a living. They were entirely dependent on others. This plight serves as the backdrop of the entire biblical book of Ruth, for example.

To that end, the Lord provided for widows and orphans and sojourners through gleaning (Leviticus 19:9 and following), the law of the first fruits (Exodus 23:19, 34:26), tithing (Deuteronomy 14:28–29), and provision for the Levites who were a total welfare people in perpetuity having no means of earning an income (Deuteronomy 14:27). The strong point to be made is that the biblical concept of justice was an economic term of equitable distribution of wealth and the opportunity to earn a living, and the people of God were to model this for the world. This aspect of caring for even the poorest people of Israel was integral to the life of the people of God. It is traced back to the commandment to be creators, curators, and cultivators.

Even in the most basic matter of sin, the biblical concept of sin is not merely having our moral failings of lying and stealing and lust washed from us but restoring the right decisions and actions toward those around us. For example, a beautiful passage regarding the cleansing of our sin is Isaiah 1:18,

"Come, let's consider your options," says the Lord. "Though your sins have stained you like the color red, you can become white like snow; though they are as easy to see as the color scarlet, you can become white like wool."

However, this verse is often cited to the neglect of the two verses immediately preceding it,

Wash! Cleanse yourselves! Remove your sinful deeds from my sight. Stop sinning. Learn to do what is right. Promote justice. Give the oppressed reason to celebrate. Take up the cause of the orphan. Defend the rights of the widow.

This is the complete life, *The Integral Life,* the people of God are supposed to demonstrate to the world. It is in the web of interdependence on one another that we can show that our hearts are cleansed from sin and white as snow. It is because of the restoration of our sense of justice toward fellow people that we can reveal the true impact of a life transformed by the Messiah.

Care-full Work

"Conservatives conserve. Where did we get the idea that conservatives exploit for capitalistic gain?"

– Ronald Reagan

We've looked at the economic example of Abraham's descendants in their blessing of all nations, but there are many other areas of care and maintenance we would be remiss to overlook. Let us return now to Genesis 2:15 and the original command from the Garden of Eden: "*to care for it and to maintain it.*" We cannot neglect the literal commission to care for the land and to maintain it. Creation care was one of our first jobs, and it modeled the care that God showed for us. He cared for and nurtured us by caring for and nurturing the growth of a garden. When we do likewise, we model the image of God written into our very nature. This extends from the literal act of caring for and maintaining plants and animals (farming) to the extent of caring for and maintaining the environment we live in.

Regarding this point, I should note my disdain of the words "environment" or "environmentalism" in this context because of their insufficient encapsulation of the command God gave humans. In short, our concern is not for a godless environment that is merely a product of the wild chance of evolution. Indeed, the end result of such an atheistic perspective is nihilism which undermines the value judgment that such environmentalism is good at all. If there is no God, it doesn't matter one whit whether the environment is destroyed and all humans are made extinct. There is no moral basis for choosing the persistence of the human species rather than choosing its extinction.

Instead, *because we are made in the image of God to care for and maintain the earth*, we must do all we can to ensure we are not destroying the earth. We do not have this concern for "Mother Earth" or because we want to help "Mother Nature." *The reason for our care and concern for Creation is that we were made stewards of that Creation.* That being the case, Creation Care is a much more accurate description than environmentalism, and Creation is a much more accurate word than the environment.

Indeed, Creation Care is a spiritual matter. We see this spiritual act not only in Genesis but in such passages as Proverbs 12:10, "*A righteous person cares for the life of his animal, but even the most compassionate acts of the wicked are cruel,*" and with a much more stern warning in Revelation 11:18,

> *The nations were enraged, but your wrath has come, and the time has come for the dead to be judged, and the time has come to give to your servants, the prophets, their reward, as well as to the saints and to those who revere your name, both small and great, and the time has come to destroy those who destroy the earth.*

Let me confess that I was a climate change skeptic. I attributed the rise in average global temperatures to cyclical changes that happen because of a variety of causes. For instance, the sun has a cyclical pattern of sunspots that repeats roughly every eleven years. I attributed changes to natural cycles similar to that.

I also conjectured that our scientific records of temperature only extend back to the 1800s, so there may have been even warmer periods well before the 1800s that we are unaware of. Humans did not have the scientific equipment or understanding of temperature metrics to make the sort of claims that humans were causing global climate change.

Additionally, catastrophic events such as volcanic eruptions or earthquakes can shift the Earth's axial tilt because of the displacement of tectonic plates. I didn't have a scientific basis for this, but I attributed the possibility of climate change to major changes from these sorts of events that may be displacing just the right mass of the Earth's core to cause an increase in observed global temperatures.

Regarding the notion of global warming, some may posit, "What hubris to think that we could affect the environment of the Earth!" In answer to that, we have shown repeatedly that we can affect the whole of Creation. The example of acid rain caused by two centuries of burning coal for heating and energy production is one instance to consider. Similarly, we observe the bleaching of coral around the world through pollution. We destroyed much of Florida's massive shrimp population with unabated draining of freshwater into the productive inter-coastal waters. We produced dead lakes like Lake Erie through irrigation runoff, and we extended the thawing of permafrost and melting glaciers that exposed mountain tops for the first time. Dismissing the ability of humans to affect Creation is simply unfounded.

Personally, in the late 1990s, I was confronted with the evidence of ice cores from the Antarctic. These ice cores, which are drilled from glaciers, catalog millennia of annual patterns of freezing and thawing of ice and snow with the seasons. These bands of visible patterns can be correlated to known times of history that correspond to especially cold or especially warm years. They can also be correlated to tree ring growth patterns elsewhere which are a record of the same.

I found that evidence compelling that we do, in fact, have a record of warming and cooling trends going back thousands of years. Though we don't know all of the contributing factors globally, I want to pay heed to warning signs that seem to show that we have not cared for Creation as we should have, whether those changes are global or more localized. Even so, my personal conviction of the readings of ice cores and tree rings doesn't matter. What matters is the injunction from Scripture to care for and maintain Creation.

My aim in this book is not to persuade readers that we are responsible for observed global warming. Nonetheless, with such a stern warning as that cited earlier from Revelation 11:18, the followers of God should be most concerned of anyone that we are *not* numbered among those destroyers of the Earth. Our injunction to care for and maintain Creation should drive us to ascertain that we are not causing global climate change through indiscriminate abuse of the resources we were made to steward.

Are humans causing global climate change? Because I am a follower of God, I should be most zealous to find out. Because I am a follower of God, I should be most zealous to be sure I am not contributing to the destruction of what is entrusted to me. I have a spiritual drive to know that I am not abusing the gifts God has given me to care for.

Mitch Hescox and Paul Douglas draw a similar conclusion in their book *Caring for Creation: The Evangelical's Guide to Climate Change and a Healthy Environment.*[26] They are followers of Jesus. Because they follow Jesus, they use their scientific and meteorological expertise to challenge fellow believers to take up Creation care. Their conclusion is that Creation care should be a spiritual priority for every believer.

To be clear, this prioritization does not supplant care for people as the chief of God's creation. We must care for humans as those who bear the image of God, and our care for animals or plants should not be prioritized above the care of those image-bearing people. Indeed, Psalm 8:5–8 says,

---

26 Paul Douglas and Mitch Hescox, *Caring for Creation: The Evangelical's Guide to Climate Change and a Healthy Environment* (Minneapolis, MN: Bethany House Publishers, 2016).

You made them a little less than the heavenly beings.

You crowned mankind with honor and majesty.

you appoint them to rule over your creation;

you have placed everything under their authority,

including all the sheep and cattle,

as well as the wild animals,

the birds in the sky, the fish in the sea,

and everything that moves through the currents of the seas.

So, care of plants and animals does not supersede care of people, but it is, nonetheless, a spiritual activity that is an injunction from the Lord. Indeed, we cannot claim to obey the whole counsel of God without caring for and maintaining Creation.

Cultivation Conclusion

Cultivation, then, is providing everything necessary for surviving and thriving. It is through obedience to the Lord's command to care for and maintain the earth, and it is through the Lord's example that we find meaning in our role as his image-bearers. The Lord cultivated a garden for our good.

That care entails obeying and modeling God's commands for

justice and rightly distributing wealth even to the poor and most needy. That care also entails resistance to the world's temptations to hoard wealth, making the rich richer and the poor poorer. That care even entails the spiritual work of Creation Care, which fulfills not only the command of God to care for and maintain his Creation but the model of what God did for us in planting a garden and placing Adam and Eve in that garden. We are cultivators who care for and maintain plants, animals, and all the earth. In doing this, we exemplify the unique image of God we are created in.

CHAPTER 6—RADICAL INTERDEPENDENCE

#MeshOfMercy

Radical Independence

On no special day in 1986, twenty-year-old Christopher Thomas Knight walked into the woods of Maine. He didn't leave for the next twenty-seven years.

Chris Knight later explained his reasoning to author Michael Finkel: he enjoyed his own company. He didn't feel the need to talk to others, so he never uttered a single word to anyone during all of those years except one hiker he passed on a trail in the 1990s when he said, "Hi."

He survived the intense cold of the Maine winter without making a fire even once. As Finkel records in his book, *The Stranger in the Woods: The Extraordinary Story of the Last True Hermit*, he never left a footprint outside of his camp for that entire time from 1986 to 2013 because footprints would allow people to find him. He deftly stepped from stone to patch of grass to stone weaving his way through the woods even in the dark.

This story seems like absolute independence. Christopher Knight declared to the world that he was going to live a life completely independent of other human beings. Except he wasn't.

Christopher Knight was alone and lived in intense solitude, but, in fact, he was totally dependent on other people. His only means of survival through all of those years was through over 1,000 burglaries in cabins and camps around two lakes. Even though his identity was unknown, he became known in the surrounding area as the North Pond Hermit, the Ghost, and even the Ninja.

These burglaries were not about money, things of value, or about getting rich. He didn't even steal money or jewelry that had been left out in the open. He didn't trash these places. Rather, he became very adept at filing open the locks of windows and rifling through refrigerators, freezers, and storage bins, gathering meat, cheese, sleeping bags, marshmallows, and candy. He had a sweet tooth! Even Chris Knight, "the last great hermit," was totally dependent on people.

We've already seen how the Tower of Babel is similar to Christopher Knight's story in that it was our societal declaration of independence, like his departure from society was his personal declaration of independence. Even so, the punishment of the Tower of Babel, namely, the confusion of languages, affects virtually every aspect of every life through every epoch. The irony of this is the extreme interdependence we have on one another because of language. To put it another way, language is the first cultural good that is passed along in our interdependence, and we are critically dependent on language to communicate with each other in order to live out all other aspects of culture. The disparity of languages is an ironic consequence of humankind thumbing their nose at the Creator in their attempt at independence from God.

The biblical cultural mandate has withstood numerous philosophical attacks through the centuries, but without doubt, the philosophy of Jean-Jacques Rousseau has had a broad influence on challenging the cultural mandate in the minds of many other philosophers. Robespierre, Marx, Lenin, Mussolini, Hitler, and

Mao were all deeply affected by Rousseau's work. In his view, "man is by nature good, and...only our institutions have made him bad."[27] As he states in his most influential work, *The Social Contract,* "Man is born free, and everywhere he is in chains." For Rousseau, the voluntary submission to society's really oppressive relationships such as marriage, family, church, and workplace corrupted what was otherwise pure and innocent humanity. One author summarizes his thinking this way,

> *This explains why it was so revolutionary when Rousseau proposed that individuals are the sole ultimate reality. He denounced civilization, with its social conventions, as artificial and oppressive. And what would liberate us from this oppression?*
>
> *The state. The state would destroy all social ties, releasing the individual from loyalty to anything except itself. Rousseau spelled out his vision with startling clarity: "Each citizen would then be completely independent of all his fellow men, and absolutely dependent on the state."*[28]

This is the natural outcome of radical independence, where the individual is set free from dependence on all other cultural institutions. Radical independence of the individual leads to anarchy in society were it not for radical dependence on the state.

---

27 Samuel Enoch Stumpf, *Philosophy: History & Problems* (New York, NY: McGrawHill, 1989), 293.

28 Nancy Pearcey, *Total Truth: Liberating Christianity from Its Cultural Captivity* (Wheaton, IL: Crossway Books, 2008), 138.

By way of a biological analogy, removal of all other bonds of assigned purpose leaves a stem cell of the individual in the same way as people who are stripped of culture and purpose. This stem cell is wholly dependent on the body for meaning and purpose. Likewise, the individual becomes wholly dependent on the state for meaning, morality, or the lack thereof. Just as the stem cell becomes whatever type of cell the body assigns it to, the individual has no purpose, meaning, or morality of one's own. The only purpose is to serve the state in whatever manner and under whatever morality the state deems appropriate. Consequently, this philosophy resulted in the bloodiest regimes of the 20th century through the aforementioned dictators, where the states act with impunity, devoid of any moral compass.

Radical Dependence

In sharp contrast to that, consider the teaching of Richard Foster. Just as we have done, Foster first looks back to Creation to note the cultural mandate to work. He, likewise, ties that to the dependence we have on one another in relationship:

> *The radical dependence of the entire creation upon God is a central teaching of this breathtaking narrative, and certainly the pivotal notion for our understanding of simplicity. We have no independent existence, no self-sustaining ability. All we are and all we possess is derived.*

> *We need to lift high the biblical doctrine of creation today, particularly our own creatureliness. We are not the captains of our souls nor the masters of our fates. We are part of the created order*

> *and hence totally dependent. Our posture is not one of arrogant acquisition, but of simple trust. What we have or ever will have comes from his gracious hand.*[29]

As Foster drills down to the thesis of his book's focus on simplicity, he exposes the dangers of work as a means of simply gathering more:

> *The idolatry of affluence is rampant. Our greed for more dictates so many of our decisions. Notice how the fourth commandment of the Sabbath rest strikes at the heart of this everlasting itch to get ahead. We find it so very hard to rest when, by working, we can get the jump on everyone else.*[30]

Foster is right to note that all of creation is *radically dependent* on God. Indeed, the author of Hebrews writes,

> *...In these last days he has spoken to us in a son, whom he appointed heir of all things, and through whom he created the world. The Son is the radiance of his glory and the representation of his essence, and he sustains all things by his powerful word, and so when he had accomplished cleansing for sins, he sat down at the right hand of the Majesty on high.*
>
> (1:2–3)

---

29 Richard J. Foster, *Freedom of Simplicity: Revised Edition: Finding Harmony in a Complex World* (New York, NY: HarperOne, 2010), 19.

30 Ibid., 20.

Similarly, Luke records Paul's words from his sermon in Acts 17:28:

> *For in him we live and move about and exist.*

Our dependence on God is no surprise. However, this dependence on God is substantially different from the relationships we have in society with other people. God has given us work, and he has equipped us to do that work. He has provided a bountiful environment where we have all we need to thrive and prosper in our work. This provision from God includes the dependence we have on one another in society. That being said, the dependence we have on one another is not codependency. This unhealthy dependence disables us as individuals and cripples a healthy society.

The dysfunction of codependency in our human relationships would result in two major problems. The first is a failure in the function of the gifts God has given us. God, in his leadership over us, has given us an environment to draw these gifts out for the valuable exercise of those gifts. The best leaders are not those who do all the necessary work themselves or even those who keep followers dependent on the leader. These would be dysfunctional leaders.

Rather, God demonstrates his role as the best sort of leader by giving his followers both the opportunity and the environment to perform their best work. These leaders draw the best out of people by recognizing their unique contributions and making space for those people to succeed.

The second problem is that living in codependency would leave our God-given potential untapped. God has given us all gifts to do the work we are called to do. If we short-circuit those gifts by unnatural overdependence on just one person, resources are left unused. We are then disenfranchised from the opportunity to do our best work and make our greatest contribution.

Radical Interdependence

What I propose here builds on Foster's recognition of our dependence on God with the recognition that we all fulfill the cultural mandate. God's first mission for humankind is to reflect his image. The most prominent ways we reflect his image are through the same line of actions He himself had done up to that point in the Creation narrative. He had created. We are creators. He had curated. We are curators. He cultivated growth. We are cultivators.

Indeed, all of the moral work we do in our occupations reflects the image of God. Reflecting God's image in our occupations demonstrates the radical interdependence that we have on one another. We are dependent on others to fulfill their created design so that we can enjoy all the benefits of society and culture. In much the same way, they are dependent on us to fulfill our created design so that they can enjoy all the benefits of society and culture.

What I present as a biblical answer to *radical independence* is akin to Foster's *radical dependence* on God because it is, in fact, the fulfillment of our created purpose within that radical dependence on God. *Radical interdependence* is the best understanding of the cultural mandate and how it is lived out through our work, our marriages, our families, our friendships, and our churches. Of course, God is not dependent on us, but we are not independent of God or of one another. We are interdependent on each other because we trust others to do things that we simply cannot do, whether this is because of nature, skill, time, or resources. In turn, we do things that they cannot do in each of those domains of life. This radical interdependence defines our sense of worth and dignity because it binds us and engages us in relationships and culture.

The contrast, then, is hubris and independence compared to humility and interdependence. The contrast is making a name for self and what "I've done" compared to making a name for God by obeying what he commanded. To put it in terms used earlier, through radical interdependence, everyone is fully equipped, everyone is fully utilized, and everyone is fulfilled. Purpose, meaning, and morality retain their rightful position as coming from God himself and being lived out through obedient followers of God.

Radical interdependence, then, is where we see our best lives lived out, and that begins in the commission of work of Genesis 1 and 2 that we call the creation mandate. It is through this mesh of mercy that we support one another and find that we, ourselves, are supported in a relationship.

CHAPTER 7–WORK AS WITNESS

#SoGoodTheyCantIgnoreYou

Subduing Cockroaches

How do we subdue and rule over cockroaches? It's unlikely that you've ever lain awake at night trying to answer this mystery of life, and it's just as unlikely that any theology professor has posed this question to budding pastors, ministers, and Bible translators. Still, it is a legitimate question. At its basic elements, the question is an extrapolation of our mandate to subdue and exercise dominion over all creation.

If it were up to me, I'd spray them all into oblivion. My first book, *Mondays in the Middle East: The Lighter Side of Arabian Nights,* recounts my unabashed disgust with cockroaches. On the other hand, a good friend of mine recognizes they are God's creatures, and he's even had the task of *training cockroaches.*

My friend, Ron Breeding, worked as an animal trainer for various education programs, stage shows, movies, and television programs. He and his wife, Shane, were regularly known in their neighborhood for bringing home all manner of interesting creatures to continue the positive reinforcement training day and night. In fact, it was not uncommon for neighbors to call on them to help wrangle an unwelcome snake or even a stray goat wandering the neighborhood. It wasn't their goat, but it was brought to their door because "who else would it belong to?"

As one example of subduing all creatures, Ron was once working for a film production company to train young chimpanzees for movie and television work. Much like raising a child, chimps require constant care until around two years of age. Trainers would take them home each night and then back to work the next day.

On this particular occasion, the chimp was happily playing on the couch one morning while Shane was in the kitchen and Ron was upstairs. An unexpected woman knocked on the screen door to share as a Jehovah's Witness, but the young chimp was the only one in the room by the door. With the doorbell as a cue, it jumped up to "welcome" the unsuspecting visitor with hoots and hollers and fist thumping. The woman screamed, "*El Diablo!*" It's unlikely this woman ever returned to their neighborhood because of the small, hairy "devil child" she met that day.

Ron and Shane's work of training animals was an exercise in subduing creation. In fact, the work Ron did on film and production sets gave these animals human-like personalities long before CGI or animatronics were in vogue. And yes, Ron was even called on to train cockroaches. This just seemed to be too much for my mind to grasp, so I asked him further, how does one go about training cockroaches? His answer: the same way Ron trains a dog or a cat or sloth or a bird. He rewards the behavior he wants and ignores the behaviors that he doesn't want. In the case of cockroaches, the reward is a drop of sugar water.

Through this approach of positive reinforcement, even a cockroach can be trained to appear as though it just graduated with honors from Juilliard. It is a matter of bringing order to chaos, turning from wildness to orderly intention.

I listened with rapt attention as Ron and Shane told these stories that exhibit amazing patience, discipline, and skill that they are too humble to claim for themselves but are abundantly obvious in each of them. It was no surprise at all when I heard that Ron was offered a position as director of a zoo. This new job would take them away from their stable, "dream" jobs in Florida, but nonetheless, they packed up life as they had known it and moved across the country.

Unfortunately, this amazing job as zoo director grew sour rather quickly. It became apparent that the park superintendent had no intention of allowing Ron to run the zoo in any way other than her way. Ron cared about the animals and the staff, and when it became clear that the superintendent's micromanagement was a harm to them, he resigned his position as zoo director with conflicted emotions and took a manufacturing job at a nearby Subaru factory.

I have to confess that, as his friend, I did not see the positives that Ron saw. I saw an incredibly talented animal trainer and leader with amazing, specialized skills that were being "wasted" on the assembly line of an auto manufacturing plant.

Even so, Ron stayed faithful to what God put in front of him. He didn't wallow in self-pity. Rather, he worked faithfully as to the Lord and not to men, whether that was using his skills as an animal trainer or making widgets for cars. Ron was a consistent worker and committed leader, and people noticed.

Over the next three years, Ron moved from Line Associate to Back-Up Team Leader to Group Leader because people recognized the faithfulness in his work ethic. His team continued to excel in the factory, and I don't think it was because he rewarded them with sugar water like cockroaches. Ron exemplified leadership. He worked with faithfulness at what the Lord put before him.

There are a number of lessons to be drawn from Ron's story.

First, of all of the people I know who have a specialized skill and a reason to pursue his passion, Ron was that person. He could have dug in his heels and made a major issue of the injustice he experienced at the zoo. He could have sat idly by collecting unemployment checks while waiting for another dream job that would use his specialized skills and passion. Instead, Ron humbly set that aside but remained faithful.

Second, he saw the need in his community, and he did his part in meeting that need. The community had a manufacturing plant where his skills could be used, so he let that need steer his course.

Third, he recognized the intrinsic value of all work. He didn't esteem a manufacturing job as lesser value or beneath him with his qualifications. In fact, now that his oldest son is of driving age, he is driving a Subaru, so there is a vested interest in excellence at work!

Finally, Ron worked to the Lord and not for men. Read these verses from Colossians carefully in light of Ron's story:

> *Whatever you are doing, work at it with enthusiasm, as to the Lord and not for people, because you know that you will receive your inheritance from the Lord as the reward. Serve the Lord Christ.*
>
> *Colossians 3:23*

Ron did not need to become a "full-time minister" such as a pastor or missionary to serve Jesus full-time. His work ethic itself was a testimony to others, and it has opened doors in spiritual matters because of the excellence of his work. His work is a witness, and he capitalizes on those opportunities "*always [being] ready to give an answer to anyone who asks about the hope you possess...*" (1 Peter 3:15).

Work Has Intrinsic Value

The idea of an *intrinsic value approach* to work looks at the needs in the community, then emphasizes the particular gift mix and abilities of the individual. No longer is the individual merely a time clock employee at the factory, but the individual represents a unique contribution that no one else can make. Of course, when this is exercised in an individual's craft as an apprentice, journeyman, and master, the individual's contribution to the outcome is obvious. When an incredibly ornate necklace is crafted by a silversmith, no one else could have made it exactly as that individual did. That being said, this sort of craft is now extremely rare, and it would be unrealistic to call for a return solely to craftsmanship.

Rather, the aim is to *redeem the individual's contribution to the outcome of the work.* For example, businesspeople, manufacturers, and software developers will immediately recognize process improvement movements such as Six Sigma, Lean Manufacturing, Kaizen, Agile Project Management, and Agile Development. Human Resource teams will immediately recognize personality tests such as the Myers-Briggs Type Indicator, LIFO, and StrengthsFinder that are used to identify the unique, personal contribution employees can make in their trade. All of these approaches and principles buttress the individual's unique contribution to the end result.

As such, these approaches begin to approximate the integration of faith and work, but—and this is key—*without the component of faith, it is impossible to recognize and reproduce God's created design for work.* We will see this in coming chapters where we focus on the tight integration, or radical interdependence, in marriage, family, friendship, and the Church.

A New Caliber of Workers

Work is sacred. It is sacred because it is a gift and command of God. Indeed, in it, we see the very expression of the image and likeness of God in our nature. For some reason, however, on account of the West's philosophical basis in Neo-Platonism, work is given second-rate status. It is not seen as sacred, but rather, it is considered tedious and loathsome, and physical labor, especially, is considered only for the lower classes.

Dave Sable of Samaritan's Purse gave a powerful encouragement some years ago at a conference where he based his discussion on the following refrain:

> *Whatever you are doing, work at it with enthusiasm, as to the Lord and not for people, because you know that you will receive your inheritance from the Lord as the reward. Serve the Lord Christ.*
>
> *Colossians 3:23–24*

He continued,

> *"Our work is honorable and holy because we serve the Lord Christ…However, our purpose, reward, and significance [are] not tied to what goes on out there. Rather, as Christians, we find God's blessing in the sacredness of the work itself."*

When you consider this Scripture passage, note something very carefully. Note that the Scripture passage applies to no other religion. No Muslim or Hindu or Buddhist has this injunction to work as to the Lord and not to men. No one else is serving the Lord of the universe in their work. What Paul is doing here is defining a new caliber of workers.

Regarding work, all of us know that there are some people who just don't want to do any work, no matter what it is. Their laziness is not about holding off until they can find a job to pursue a passion. It's just laziness and slothfulness.

Next, consider that there are transactional workers. These are people who will take whatever job will allow them to live the lifestyle they want. Their heart isn't in the work, and they probably couldn't care less about the work itself. Their aim is to do the least amount of work that will keep them employed.

Each of us also knows a group of people we can call career-oriented people. They do their work and they do it well because *it will lead to better and better work*. They aren't focused on gifting or meeting a need or the intrinsic value of work. They just want to perform their best so that they can get better work, whether that means more money, more power, more flexibility, less oversight, or whatever the motivation might be.

Then, we also know of another group, even outside of Christian circles, that sees its work as a part of its identity. These people see their work as their calling, so they do their best work because it defines who they are and, in fact, this might even give them a great deal of joy. They might have the satisfaction of knowing that they are making a contribution that no one else can make because only they have the particular skill-and-gift mix to accomplish the job they do.

That seems like a pretty high bar to top, but there is still one other demographic, namely, followers of Jesus. Only Christians have this injunction, "*Whatever you are doing, work at it with enthusiasm, as to the Lord and not for people.*" In fact, over and above the comparison between the Lord and men, Paul strengthens his words by stating plainly, "*You are serving the Lord Christ*" (ESV).

Think for a moment about what this means. Whatever your work is, you are serving the Lord Christ. The next chapter will address immoral work, but if your work is "honest work," you are serving the Lord Christ. If you are a landscaper, you are planting trees and flowers and cutting the lawn and running machinery for Christ. If you are a truck driver, you are abiding by traffic laws, showing courtesy and respect in driving, operating your vehicle safely because you are serving the Lord Christ. If you are responsible for monitoring water quality or invasive species in freshwater lakes, you should do this with all your heart and to the utmost of your ability because you are serving the Lord Christ.

Although he wasn't referring to the same Scriptural passage, Martin Luther King, Jr. stated something similar when he said, "If a man is called to be a street sweeper, he should sweep streets even as Michelangelo painted, or Beethoven composed music or Shakespeare wrote poetry. He should sweep streets so well that all the hosts of heaven and earth will pause to say, 'Here lived a great street sweeper who did his job well.'"[31]

The point is that Scripture defines a new caliber of workmanship because all moral work we do serves the Lord Christ.

---

31 Martin L. King, "If a Man Is Called to Be a Street Sweeper," Goodreads (Goodreads), accessed October 31, 2019, https://www.goodreads.com/quotes/21045-if-a-man-is-called-to-be-a-street-sweeper.

A New Caliber of Workers

Your Work Ethic Reflects Your Faith Epic

Regarding the intrinsic value of work, consider this example that Moses recorded in Exodus 36:

> *So Bezalel and Oholiab and every skilled person in whom the Lord has put skill and ability to know how to do all the work for the service of the sanctuary are to do the work according to all that the Lord has commanded."*
>
> *Moses summoned Bezalel and Oholiab and every skilled person in whom the Lord had put skill—everyone whose heart stirred him to volunteer to do the work. They received from Moses all the*

> *offerings the Israelites had brought to do the work for the service of the sanctuary, and they still continued to bring him a freewill offering each morning.*
>
> *Exodus 36:1–3*

Read carefully how these men and every skilled person got their skill: "*So Bezalel and Oholiab and every skilled person in whom the Lord has put skill...*" The Lord put this skill in them. The Lord enabled them to do their work with utmost care. The Lord was the one who both benefited from the beautiful craftsmanship that was exhibited and the one who put it there, to begin with. The work was not about merely getting a job done. It was about making a contribution to the world through the skill that God himself had put in these people.

Another passage that relates a similar idea comes from just a few chapters earlier in this instruction from God to Moses:

> *You must make holy garments for your brother Aaron, for glory and for beauty.*
>
> *Exodus 28:2*

God's instruction makes clear that it was not just about getting a job done. He didn't say, "Yeah, I suppose you should make some clothes for Aaron and his sons." The craftsmanship that the Lord required was nothing short of glorious and beautiful.

Now, couple this information about the intrinsic value of work with the discussion about our role as culture makers. One point from that discussion was that none of us starts from a clean slate regarding culture. We have culture that is passed on to us, and with that culture, we make something of the world. Bezalel and Oholiab and these other artisans had deep cultural roots that went back generations that would have taught them the collective wisdom to excel at their craft. Bezalel didn't decide to take a two-week seminar on masonry and suddenly find himself an expert. Oholiab didn't take a course on carpentry so that he would be equipped to build the ornate woodcraft of the tabernacle. Moses did not pick up skills as a tailor through a side gig to make a little extra cash and then qualify to make Aaron's garments "*for glory and for beauty.*" In each of these cases, what we know about artisans of the Old Testament period indicates that these skills were passed on and perfected through generations so that when the people got to the time frame of the Exodus, they created something magnificent.

Through all of this, you could say that their work ethic reflected their faith epic. The degree to which they did their work well was the degree of their devotion to their faith. Running roughshod over the work to finish a mediocre job was not an option. The Jewish culture was a culture that respected the intrinsic value of work.

As a sampling of Scripture that reinforces this, consider the following:

> *Commit your works to the Lord, and your plans will be established.*
>
> *Proverbs 16:3*

> *You have seen a person skilled in his work—he will take his position before kings; he will not take his position before obscure people.*
>
> *Proverbs 22:29*

There is nothing better for people than to eat and drink, and to find enjoyment in their work. I also perceived that this ability to find enjoyment comes from God...

Ecclesiastes 2:24

And whatever you do in word or deed, do it all in the name of the Lord Jesus, giving thanks to God the Father through him.

Colossians 3:17

... Showing yourself to be an example of good works in every way. In your teaching show integrity, dignity, and a sound message that cannot be criticized, so that any opponent will be at a loss, because he has nothing evil to say about us.

Titus 2:7–8

You yourselves know that these hands of mine provided for my needs and the needs of those who were with me. By all these things, I have shown you that by working in this way we must help the weak, and remember the words of the Lord Jesus that he himself said, 'It is more blessed to give than to receive.'"

Acts 20:34–35

The one who steals must steal no longer; instead he must labor, doing good with his own hands, so that he will have something to share with the one who has need.

Ephesians 4:28

For you as well, do you see your work as part of your faith story? From Genesis 1 and forward, the Bible expects that your work is part of your faith story. Your work ethic reflects your faith epic. The value you place on work is part of your faith story.

CHAPTER 8–
OCCUPATIONAL HAZARDS

#CorruptIntent

Did Ely Whitney Assassinate Abraham Lincoln?

The seasons are changing at the time of this writing, so people are abandoning their short summer clothes and donning long sleeves and long slacks. Of course, there are all sorts of fabrics to suit your fancy. Some years ago, I found some dress slacks that used nanotechnology to amazing effect. The nanotechnology prevented wrinkles, prevented odor, prevented stains, etc. I affectionately nicknamed them my "Robo-pants" since it seemed they could do everything short of walking by themselves.

Over the past 200 years, though, one fabric has dominated the clothing industry bar none, and that fabric is cotton. Before the turn of the 18th to 19th centuries, most people had but one set of clothes or maybe two. On the other hand, in 1793, the young inventor Eli Whitney mechanized the removal of seeds from the picked cotton so that cotton as a fabric could be mass-produced. As I sit today in my Wrangler© jeans, I celebrate the achievement of this young man and the creative brilliance he brought to the world of clothing.

In that same era, another notable creation came into being, namely, the United States of America. I celebrate the freedoms affirmed in the Declaration of Independence from Great Britain of 1776 and the writing of the Constitution of 1787. Again, I recognize brilliance in much of what is written in the documents that were used to establish and found this country.

Recently, I was listening to lectures on U.S. history, and I learned something about the stain of slavery that mars our country's history. I was surprised to learn that many of our country's founders felt that slavery was a relic of days gone by and that eventually, it would simply die out in the newly established United States because demand would simply go away. The reasoning behind this waning demand was that the US did not have a mono-cultural crop that necessitated slavery. For example, there was a mono-culture in Virginia with tobacco, but it was not large enough, and the demand was not great enough to necessitate slave labor to maintain it. Likewise, there was a mono-culture of sugar cane in the Caribbean, but again, sugar was a supplemental crop, not a staple that would necessitate a massive force of labor to sustain it. So, lacking a mono-culture crop, the founding fathers felt that within a generation or two, slavery would simply die of its own accord without the need to eliminate it by writ through the Constitution.

Who among the founding fathers could have foreseen the near-simultaneous creation of the spinning gin and the cotton gin only six years after the adoption of the Constitution that would change the American landscape forever? In fact, Eli Whitney himself could not have presumed to know the explosive impact of his invention on this infant country. His aim was simply to make the extraction of the cotton seeds less painful and arduous and, frankly, less bloody for the few cotton farmers that labored in these fields.

On the other hand, what Eli Whitney created was the possibility of durable, cheap textiles for everyone from Europe through the Americas. As a result of his invention, the price of textiles dropped an astounding ninety-nine percent. Cotton, then, became the mono-cultural crop that was missing from the American landscape. This mono-cultural crop required an intensive labor force which necessitated and drove a market for cheap labor, namely, slavery. In hindsight, of course, we know that slavery alone nearly tore this country in two through the Civil War, which was anything but civil. It even resulted in the assassination of one of the most influential presidents this country has known.

So, the question is, was Eli Whitney responsible for the Civil War? Was he responsible for the assassination of Abraham Lincoln? After all, it was his innovation that made both events possible.

A Broken Foundation

When we look at the way we bear the image of God as creators, curators, and cultivators, we recognize that each new cultural good makes some things possible and other things impossible. The construction of barbed-wire fencing used across the plains of the western United States made it possible for ranchers to allow cattle to roam freely with relative safety. That same cultural good made it impossible for wild bison to range freely across the same land as they had for centuries. Depending on the perspective, then, those possibilities and impossibilities can be good or bad. Even more, some innovations are intended for evil from their very creation. These are not good and might not be redeemable at all in their function. These cultural products reflect the corruption of work.

Consider the *Telos Tower* as it was presented in earlier chapters. The very basis and foundation of the *Telos Tower* is the glory of God. The sinful act of removing the glory of God as the foundation and replacing it, for example, with the glory of Bill Gates or the glory of Richard Dawkins, destroys the foundation of the *Telos Tower*. Richard Dawkins' books that rationalize unbelief in God are a sinful cultural good. Bill Gates' philanthropy to prevent malaria as a humanist endeavor has no inherent meaning or value because he does not even recognize his own created design. Richard Dawkins may use his creative, innovative skills from God as a writer and speaker, but he is corrupting those skills by exalting himself and declaring himself an enemy of God while denying God's created design of art, order, and care. Bill Gates may exercise his gifts of care for people to provide the best environment conducive to growth, but he is undermining the God who gave him those gifts by denying the created design of art, order, and care. Just because a person's gifts manifest the image of art, order, and care doesn't indicate that the end result of their cultural product is inherently good. The gifts are good, but the intent can be corrupted by sin. In this way, the use of Eli Whitney's cotton gin for the exploitation of over six million slaves in the United States was not morally good, even though it was a use of the innovative image of God built into each of us.

One of the outstanding aspects of the Bible that demonstrates its truth is that it admits the sinful actions of people, even of its own "heroes." This aspect of the Bible is unlike other religious books that merely glamorize and idolatrize their "heroes." That being the case, we can see many corruptions of our created purpose and corruptions of our work. Even considering the other domains of *the integral life,* such as marriage, family, friendship, and the Church, the Bible recounts failings in each of these, so it presents a very candid, honest portrayal of the human condition that doesn't take a superhero to relate to. The Bible is for everyday people, including in its description of the corruption of God's created design.

Even when considering work alone, there are many corruptions that we can identify in the Bible. We see prostitution with Rahab and Judah's sin with his daughter-in-law, Tamar. There are explorations of carnal pleasures that include Solomon's 700 wives and 300 concubines. Another man gambles his daughter's life away to win a battle. There are nauseating stories of rape and murder that have stopped readers in their tracks.

Perhaps a not-so-humorous story from my own family is one that my mother tells of her grandmother. Her grandmother wanted to take her faith more seriously, so she decided to read the Bible straight through, starting with Genesis. She read as far as Judges before she stopped reading and simply put it down because of the distasteful content. She still followed the Christian faith, but she didn't read the Bible.

Are these examples of wickedness any different from our own time? Without even knowing the specific instances, I could ask a college student, "Would you say we are closer to zero percent similar to the Old Testament sins today or closer to fifty percent? Are we closer to fifty percent or closer to eighty percent similar? Are we more like eighty percent similar or ninety-five percent similar in the terrible things done today compared to Old Testament times?" I think the conclusion would be that we are very close to one-hundred percent similar to the sins of the Old Testament times, with the only exception being the instruments of evil being used for sin today. We are more advanced in the tools for sin, but the fact of human depravity is very much the same. Human depravity has caused human work to be used for human sin.

Occupational Hazards

On our own, we break the foundation in the *Telos Tower*, without a doubt. That broken foundation affects everything above it, including our approach to our work and occupations. The broken foundation that serves us instead of God will corrupt the Art we produce so that our hedonism and pleasure become the focus of our creative work. The broken foundation will corrupt the *ordering* of our world so that we convince ourselves, for example, that the incredibly complex design we see in the universe is a product of random chance and evolutionary mutations rather than the handiwork of the Creator. This broken foundation leads us to exploit, for example, the tremendous resources the Lord has given to provide for us at the expense of the very environment we live in.

When the foundation is marred, corruption eats through the entire tower tainting the very work we were made to do. In fact, work becomes another point of resistance against God. We simply do not want to do what he has commanded us to do. Laziness becomes our drive because we do not want to work. Gambling becomes our drive because we think we can get the benefits of work without doing the work. Injustice becomes our drive because we find ways to exploit others so that we get the benefits of work without having to do the work. Greed becomes our motivation because we live under the false belief that if we just have enough, we won't need to work anymore. As America's first billionaire, John D. Rockefeller, was once asked by a reporter, "How much money is enough?" He replied, "Just a little bit more."[32]

Consider the woman who does her accounting work well with care and clarity. However, she establishes a fund that directs money outside of the organization's normal revenue streams to funnel money directly to herself. This embezzlement and fraud do not reflect God's glory, but they reflect her own greed and malice. The tower collapses under its weight because God's glory

32 Steven Haynes, Starwinar website https://starwinar.wordpress.com/daily-short-story/just-a-little-bit-more/ accessed April 14, 2022.

has been removed, and no matter how well she does her accounting, it is a sin because of this corruption.

Indeed, the tower collapses if any of the areas of our representation of God on earth are corrupted. If someone manifests his rule and dominion over Creation and lives that out through Mountaintop Removal Mining so that the mountain is destroyed and the water supply is polluted in the valley below, his rule over Creation is sin. He has not cared for and maintained Creation. The tower collapses under the weight of this sin.

Similarly, if a lawyer uses exceptional skills of reason and astute reading of the law to allow a murderer to go free, this perversion of justice does not reflect the image of God in her. The complete disregard of the victim being made in the image of God causes the glory of God to be marred, distorted, and corrupted. The tower collapses.

Furthermore, there are other corruptions of work that are not necessarily moral corruptions but rather corruptions of motives. For example, someone may use a job as an escape from a difficult situation at home. Rather than face the problem at home and exhibit leadership in the household by addressing the issue at hand, he works more hours taking more time away from his wife and children. When these priorities are confused and this becomes habitual, we call it workaholism.

We can see corruption in work by looking at forced labor under communist rule. When Aleksandr Solzhenitsyn describes the labor camps of Siberia in *The Gulag Archipelago*, the inhumane treatment of people and of prisoners is not a model of work. It is a corruption of work.

Leading a gossip campaign against a colleague in order to tear him down and build yourself up is not an example of an excellent employee who really "grabs the bull by the horns to get the job done." It is a corruption of work. Even doing this at a Christian organization doesn't make it any less of a sin. Rather, it is even more reprehensible considering the testimony of righteousness and justice expected to exist in the organization.

Carnal pleasures are a seemingly ubiquitous corruption of work. Brittni De La Mora is a beautiful example of the Lord's redeeming work in this area. Brittni is a former porn star who made the decision to follow Jesus after seven years of hearing the team from XXXChurch.com telling her that Jesus loved her. Brittni's website records more of her story,

> *[Brittni] was once named one of the world's most famous porn stars. At the pinnacle of her career in the adult entertainment industry, she had acquired fame, money, and success by having landed over 250-plus roles in film. However, the prominent memories she recalls during this time were the deepest, darkest days of despair, leading her to survive by way of drugs, alcohol, and ultimately, failed attempts of suicide.*
>
> *Through a divine series of events, she began to encounter the love of God, which became substantial enough for her to make a dramatic, unexpected decision by all who knew her to leave the industry overnight.*[33]

Brittni's story is a life transformed by Jesus. It is an example of

---

33 Brittni De La Mora, "Brittni De La Mora," Love Always Ministries, accessed April 23, 2022, https://www.lovealwaysministries.com/brittnidelamora.

utter corruption of work and complete renewal into a new life marked by the love of God.

While putting myself through college, I took jobs through a temp agency during breaks away from my university studies. One of the jobs I was assigned to was at the printing company Quad Graphics which was located near my hometown in Wisconsin. It was well known in our area that Quad Graphics was the printer for the magazine *Playboy*. I certainly didn't want to be printing *Playboy* magazines, but I knew that Quad Graphics printed a lot of other things as well, and I showed up for work, hoping that I was assigned to some other printing work.

As it happened, I was tasked with boxing and sealing the *Playboy Christmas Edition*. Who would have thought there ever was such a thing? Celebrating the birth of the Savior with displays of naked women?! Of course, this work did not sit well with me. Producing *Playboy* magazines and enabling the sinful lust of millions of readers was something my conscience simply would not allow me to do.

In light of this, I approached my line supervisor and explained that I had moral objections to producing *Playboy* magazines, and I asked if there was another job I could be assigned to. He was sympathetic to my misgivings, so he took me to his supervisor. I explained the same thing and asked to be reassigned. He was sympathetic but bewildered by the request. He took me to the foreman. For the third time, I explained that I had moral objections to producing *Playboy* and asked if there was something else I could be assigned to. His response lacked any moral conviction, and he simply said, "Nope. Get the f—— out."

The work was corrupt, and I simply could not contribute. I was studying for degrees in Bible and Biblical Studies, preparing to be a pastor. How would I answer if someone asked me when I got back to my university, "What did you do over break?" "Printed *Playboy* magazines" would not have been the right answer under any circumstances.

This is the same advice we see from the Apostle Paul when he addresses corruption in work. He was apparently aware of a particular corruption of work even in the beloved church in Ephesus when he wrote,

> *The one who steals must steal no longer; instead he must labor, doing good with his own hands, so that he will have something to share with the one who has need.*
>
> *Ephesians 4:28*

Paul gave no rationalization for continuing to do the work. Even if the thief was a really good thief and very talented at what he did, there were no exceptions. If someone's job was stealing, he was to steal no longer.

Paul didn't merely leave it there, however. Simply saying, "Don't do that," would be like saying, "For the next minute, don't think of a pink elephant." The idea is planted there, so the person is naturally going to think of a pink elephant.

On the other hand, if someone said, "For the next minute, I only want you to think of a green elephant." After one minute, the person could be asked, "During that minute, did you think of a pink elephant?" The answer would be no because the person was thinking of a green elephant.

In like manner, Paul gives the thief, the gambler, the porn star, the embezzler, the drug dealer a path out, "*...instead he must labor, doing good with his own hands.*" Even in this, Paul has a greater purpose that leads to the state of radical interdependence we look at in this book. His purpose: "…*so that he will have something to share with the one who has need.*" Our work provides for ourselves, it provides for our families, it provides for our work, and it provides for others who might have need. *The answer to the corruption of work is moral work that honors God and demonstrates our interdependence on one another.*

SECTION 2–
CULTURE MAKERS

The expression of the creation mandate can take a number of forms, from tangible cultural goods such as roads, buildings, and cities to intangible cultural goods such as language, literacy, or family recipes. Nonetheless, these artful creations all fulfill the Lord's commands to be fruitful, multiply, and fill the earth.

It should be noted again that none of us starts with a clean cultural slate. We all inherit the cultural goods that are passed on to us by family, society, church, friends, relatives, etc. They have fulfilled the cultural mandate through their artful creation so that our starting point is well down the road, replete with vast numbers of cultural goods.

Consider for a moment the explosive power of a rocket that will propel people into orbit around the Earth. Disregard for the moment the immense number of cultural goods I've assumed in that previous sentence, such as what a rocket is, jet propulsion, orbit, overcoming the Earth's gravitational force, and so on. Instead, consider that in our generation, we inherit algebra, trigonometry, calculus, special relativity, and general relativity. What would the world be like if we did not inherit the cultural goods of those that have gone before us and we had to "reinvent the wheel" literally? We would still be scratching cave walls with stones to express our art, and we would still be throwing rocks at rabbits to express our dominion over all of the earth. Culture is necessary for us to excel as human beings. Culture is our starting point, and it is only from that starting point that we can, ourselves, begin to make culture.

That second aspect of making culture is too often understood in a very limited sense. People restrict culture to fashion innovations such as a fist bump instead of a high-five or jeggings replacing sweatpants. These surface elements of culture do not even approximate the depth of culture each of us has absorbed.

To demonstrate the depth of this culture, I'll share the innovation of Stuart Brand, which he introduced in his 1999 book *The Clock of The Long Now: Time and Responsibility*. In this book, Brand introduces Pace Layers which is a means of looking at the speed of change in society. The following graphic illustrates his concept of Pace Layers, where the layers of society that change fastest are at the top, and those that are more stable with slower change are at the bottom:

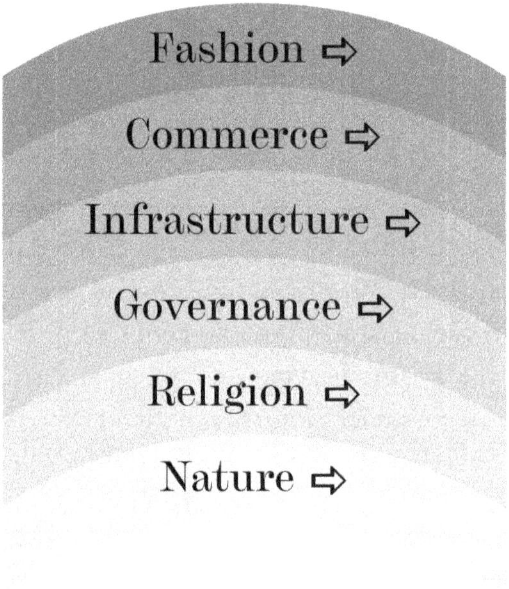

Culture in All We Do

Despite the value of noting the pace of societal change, Brand's major blunder in his taxonomy separates culture, from all of the elements of *Culture* such as nature, governance, infrastructure, commerce, fashion, and art. In fact, "religion" is an apt substitute for the word "culture" because the primary things he describes in *Culture* are religious elements. Indeed, when we consider the pace of change of religion, it fits perfectly in the layer where Brand has placed *Culture.* The graphic above reflects this improvement.

It may be contested, who am I to question the work of a brilliant futurist who thinks deeply about the Long Now and what things will be like 10,000 years from now? Without claiming any pedigree for myself, let me simply use an illustration to show that culture and infrastructure, as an example, are inseparably enmeshed and influence one another deeply.

Culture and Its Products

Consider the humble telephone. The earliest telephone I remember in our home was a rotary phone. We only had one, not one for each room. Touch-tone phones hadn't been invented, but like most families, we had one rotary phone in the home. Sharing that fact brings with it the cultural expectation that our family members knew how to use a rotary phone and, later, I learned how to use a simpler touch-tone phone as well. These were elements of my culture that would have been completely foreign in other parts of the world at that time.

Obviously, this story dates me, but I seem even more antiquated when I share that at the same time, my grandparents used a party-line phone system on their rural Wisconsin farm. For those of you whose culture did not include party lines, it takes a bit of explanation. Five to ten rural families would all be parties to the use of a single connection to the "local" phone switch. Only one party could make a call at a time. However, there was always the risk that one or more of the other parties might pick up the phone in the midst of an ongoing call and remain quiet to catch a bit of gossip. Fortunately for my grandparents, the Brauns and the Engels were trustworthy neighboring families.

That is the basic description of the telephone infrastructure of the last fifty years of the 20th century. Now let me paint a picture of the telephone infrastructure I observed while living in Oman in 2005 and how even the humble telephone is an influential product of culture.

Surprisingly, almost no one had telephones wired to their houses in Oman. There were no "telephone lines" strung from building to building and no green, local switching boxes to route calls. It was almost as though 20th-century communications had skipped Oman entirely. Yet, the people of Oman were some of the most savvy adopters of telephony that I've ever seen. How do these two worlds line up? What can this teach us about culture and infrastructure? Let me explain.

It is true that 20th-century telephony really did skip Oman for the most part and jumped directly to the 21st century. The Omani utility companies reasoned that they could skip the costly, labor-intensive effort of wiring every home with one or more phone lines. Instead, they realized they could put up one mobile phone tower and instantly make mobile telephone service available to 8,000 customers, as an example. Spacing towers every two to five kilometers throughout our village of 100,000 people allowed most of the population to have access to mobile phone service if they wanted it.

Here's the cultural key. Since these Omanis weren't bound by their cultural understanding of telephone use, they leaped far ahead of what I was familiar with in North America. The first phones many of them used were mobile phones, so they used the full capacity of mobile phones from the outset. On the other hand, Americans had been conditioned for decades that phones were for voice calls. Often, those calls were taking up limited resources (e.g., a party line), so calls were made sparingly or kept short. Even in cities where phone use was more common, phone companies marketed discounts for limited-minute phone packages of, say, 200 minutes per month. Mind you, these packages were for wired home phones, not the familiar bundle of minutes that mobile phone users might be accustomed to. Culturally, Americans were being trained that phones were for audio calls, and they were to be used infrequently.

In the desert of Arabia, that cultural conditioning and baggage were skipped. Instead, users were conditioned and rewarded for using text services (SMS). Talking on an audio call for one minute costs the same as three texts, so people naturally gravitated toward the cheaper texting option.

In short, the cultural liability of not having home phones facilitated an explosion of SMS, MMS, audio chat, video chat, and Internet telephony that launched the cities of the Middle East years ahead of the West. Even in something as fundamental as telephone infrastructure, culture is intricately entwined. Culture starts with what we are given. What we make of the world is more culture, even if that is infrastructure, commerce, fashion, and so on.

Depth of Culture in the Integral Life

Irrespective of this misnomer in Brand's taxonomy, the redeeming quality of what he has produced is recognizing the depth of culture through all of life, and the pace of change of that culture through all of life. Culture is not merely fashion and art, as many might suppose when they speak of "the culture." Culture is not monolithic, but rather, culture and the places where we grow (that is, enculture) as human beings permeate all of life. Culture is part of every aspect of the integral life.

As was referred to earlier, Andy Crouch quotes Ken Myers in his definition of culture: what we make of the world. It makes sense that this culture-making happens in all parts of life, not simply in fashion and art. What we make of the world happens in the advent of jeggings, yes, but it happens in the creation of subprime mortgages and erasable ink pens and the electoral college and in non-profit status of religious institutions. In all of these domains, we express the integral life because all of these domains together comprise the lives we live. In each of them, we can observe the same sort of interdependence we've identified in the image of God that we bear. We can see this interdependence in art, order, and care. We can see this interdependence in our roles as creators, curators, and cultivators. To be sure, our occupations and work are a model of interdependence, but they are not the sum of all interdependence. Rather, this principle is lived out in the domains of marriage, family, friendship, and in the Church, where we turn our attention to now as culture makers.

CHAPTER 9—MARRIAGE

#MutualBlessing

In my early adult years, I was looking to save money, and I didn't have many possessions or a need for a home to live in. On account of this, I rented a room from Wylma and Lloyd Buckles, an elderly couple who made use of the extra space in their family home by renting out rooms to college students. Wylma and Lloyd were a picture of contented retirement. They didn't go on fancy trips, and they didn't take up residence in a warmer state, but they remained in Minnesota even through the cold of winter. They spent their time in different hobbies like calligraphy and woodworking, and they passed along these skills to their children and their grandchildren. In short, they enjoyed each other's company and seemed to perfectly complete one another.

Some years after I moved out of their home, I received Wylma's sad news that Lloyd went to be with the Lord. Undoubtedly, this was a difficult time for Wylma as she was now living alone without her life partner, but she stayed in the same home, living the same life. Even so, only four months later, Wylma was raking leaves in her yard when she simply fell over, passed on from this life to the next. It seemed that without Lloyd, much of the life that she had known simply was not there. A major part of her life on earth had gone ahead, and with him went that purpose for continuing in this life.

For ages, people have called this sort of event "Broken Heart

Syndrome," but many medical professionals questioned whether it was, in fact, possible that a person could be so overwhelmed with grief that it would lead to death. In February of 2005, the *New England Journal of Medicine* published a study concluding that, indeed, Broken Heart Syndrome was real and deadly. A publication of Johns Hopkins Medicine summarizes, "Patients with this condition, called stress cardiomyopathy but known colloquially as 'broken heart' syndrome, are often misdiagnosed with a massive heart attack when, indeed, they have suffered from a days-long surge in adrenalin (epinephrine) and other stress hormones that temporarily 'stun' the heart."[34] For Wylma Buckles, the four monthly reminders of the date she lost her life's complement, Lloyd, were so great that they appeared to have ended her own life.

By design, the Lord created husbands and wives to be dependent on one another. We were created with different physical make-up and different emotional make-up for the purpose of representing a complete, integral whole together. In biblical terms, "*That is why a man leaves his father and mother and unites with his wife, and they become one family*" (Genesis 1:24).

That is to say that a man begins as part of the unified whole of his family of origin. He is part of one family. He then leaves that family in order to be united with his wife to establish a new family. This is the intended pattern for men and women that God created for us.

Of course, this is not to speak less of those that do not find themselves in the typical pattern. There are single adults for a variety of reasons. Although Peter lived as a married man, the

---

34 March, David. "'Broken Heart' Syndrome: Real, Potentially Deadly But Recovery Quick." Johns Hopkins Medicine, accessed April 22, 2022, https://www.hopkinsmedicine.org/press_releases/2005/02_10_05.html

Apostle Paul himself lived life as a single man, and he wished that everyone could be as he was for the sake of ministry. Nonetheless, the clear intended design taught by Paul is for a man to be united with his wife so that "*they become one family.*"

Adam and Eve certainly represent a good example of a man being united with his wife to become one family, but another couple in Scripture represents this integral unit even better in the face of alternative cultural products, namely, Abram and Sarai. Genesis 12 records how Abram was called out of his home country of Ur with the promise that God would make Abram into a great nation that would, in fact, be a blessing to all the families of the earth. As it happened, Abram's wife, Sarai, did not become pregnant, and by all accounts, it looked as though she would not be the person through which this promise would be fulfilled.

Abram ages and begins to consider the option of bequeathing his wealth to Eliezer of Damascus,

> *After these things the Lord's message came to Abram in a vision: "Fear not, Abram! I am your shield and the one who will reward you in great abundance."*
>
> *But Abram said, "O Sovereign Lord, what will you give me since I continue to be childless, and my heir is Eliezer of Damascus?" Abram added, "Since you have not given me a descendant, then look, one born in my house will be my heir!"*
>
> *But look, the Lord's message came to him: "This man will not be your heir, but instead a son who comes from your own body will be your heir." The Lord took him outside and said, "Gaze into*

> *the sky and count the stars—if you are able to count them!" Then he said to him, "So will your descendants be."*
>
> *Genesis 15:1–5*

The Lord made clear that Abram himself would produce an heir, but he could not do this on his own. Bequeathing his riches apart from a child of his own would not fulfill this promise.

Even through Sarai's misguided attempt to produce a child through her servant, Hagar, the Lord makes clear thirteen years later that Sarai (now called Sarah) would produce the son of the covenant promise,

> *God said, "No, Sarah your wife is going to bear you a son, and you will name him Isaac. I will confirm my covenant with him as a perpetual covenant for his descendants after him."*
>
> *Genesis 17:19*

Again, it is clear that God did not intend for Abram (now called Abraham) to bless the nations either as a single man or through a concubine, but solely through the integral union of Abraham and Sarah. Marriage between a man and a woman is the irreplaceable plan of God for the fulfillment of Abraham's covenant as well as the creation mandate.

An Integral Union

Sexuality, as created and defined by God, is complementary between a husband and a wife alone. A husband provides things to the union that a wife cannot, and a wife provides things to the union that a husband cannot. This provision is anatomical, of course, but it also extends to qualities and roles within the family. Indeed, Genesis 1:27 gives us an example of what is called a *tautology* which is defined as "a statement whose structure makes it true."[35] For example, "the ice cube is frozen" is a tautology. If an ice cube were not frozen, it would not be an ice cube. The structure of ice having the quality of being frozen makes the statement true by necessity.

> *God created humankind in his own image, in the image of God he created them, male and female he created them.*

In the verse of Scripture above, "*God created humankind*" is, of course, intended to be generically understood as men and women. The last phrase in the sentence makes this clear when it further elucidates, "*male and female he created them.*" That is, then, the totality of humankind: every man is male, and every woman is female. To be a man is to be a mature male, and to be a woman is to be a mature female. These are tautologies.

As only two genders of male and female, we are a species that is interdependent on one another for natural function. Attempts are being made to twist these tautologies, but these attempts simply do not correspond to reality.

---

35 Howard Kahane, *Logic and Contemporary Rhetoric the Use of Reason in Everyday Life* (Belmont, CA: Wadsworth, 1992), 311.

For husbands and wives, their complementary sexual union is the most obvious fulfillment of the commands from the Creator, "*Be fruitful and multiply and fill the earth*" (Genesis 1:28). From the very beginning, we were made interdependent on one another, and this interdependence rings true today just as it did when Adam woke up with Eve at his side. This is the integral union of God's created design.

More Than Mere Dependence

Remarkably, the man, Adam, was not solely dependent on God. When God created humanity, he could have made Adam be solely and directly dependent on God alone. However, this state of affairs was the only thing in God's creation that he concluded was not good; man was alone.

Women were necessary for God's created design of interdependence. To demonstrate this, consider that Adam's life was made to be everlasting. He had access to the tree of life before sin, and he would have lived forever were it not for sin. If Adam was intended to be solely dependent on God, creation would have been finished and complete with Adam. There would have been no need for Eve or women at all because God would have been sufficient for Adam's relationship. One man, Adam, would have lived eternally, carrying on God's commands with God as his companion.

Of course, this was not God's created intention. By the very act of fashioning Eve from Adam, we can see that even perfect dependence on God was not sufficient for God's created design of relationship. From the very beginning, God intended complementary interdependence of men and women on each other.

Of course, we can also reason that it was not functionally plausible for men to be independent of women. Only together are men and women able to reproduce. In other words, only in their interdependence on one another can they fulfill God's commands to be fruitful, multiply, and fill the earth. They were both made in the image of God, and each, respectively, was dependent on the other. Together, they made an integral union. This, and nothing short of it, is the natural function established by God.

Unnatural Desires

The marriage of Abraham and Sarah is a model of that natural function, and we read of that in the early chapters of Genesis. Even though they sinfully attempted to manipulate childbearing through polygamy with Hagar, the created design that the Lord had in mind for Abraham and Sarah was clear because the promise only came through their child, Isaac.

Humans have devised myriad corruptions of marital union. The catch-all word used often in the Bible is the Greek word *porneias*. Even though this is the word we derive "pornography" from, the word is not limited to pornography but is a general term for sexual sin, including fornication (that is, sexual relations before marriage), adultery (that is, extramarital sexual relations during marriage), homosexuality, gender choice, bestiality, or any other sexual sin.

In 2002, Courtney Wild was an impressionable fourteen-year-old girl living in Palm Beach, Florida. One of her close friends told her how she could make $200 by giving a rich man a massage. "That was more money than Courtney had ever seen. It was an easy decision, so she took a cab with [her friend] over to the rich guy's house."[36]

---

36 Bradley J. Edwards and Brittany Henderson, *Relentless Pursuit: My Fight for the Victims of Jeffrey Epstein* (New York, NY: Gallery Books, 2020), 40.

Courtney Wild's introduction to Jeffrey Epstein followed a similar predatory pattern as he recruited underage girls and groomed them to provide sexual favors for rich and famous men. His actions alone include most of the list of sins that the Apostle Paul identifies in 1 Corinthians 6:9–10,

> *Do you not know that the unrighteous will not inherit the kingdom of God? Do not be deceived! The sexually immoral, idolaters, adulterers, passive homosexual partners, practicing homosexuals, thieves, the greedy, drunkards, the verbally abusive, and swindlers will not inherit the kingdom of God.*

The inhuman practices of Jeffrey Epstein include the greedy, drunkards, abusers, swindlers, sexually immoral, and adulterers. These sins stand in opposition to the Lord's created design for marriage, and they lead to another story that is injected right into the middle of the chapters of Genesis recounting Abraham's life. That story includes the most notorious example of homosexuality in Scripture, namely, the debasing sin of Sodom and Gomorrah.

What is the impact of homosexuality? What is the impact of fornication or adultery, or any sexual sin? The gift of sexuality is a most precious gift from the Lord; who is affected by its corruption?

To be sure, everyone has sinned in many different ways. Sin is an infinite offense against an infinitely good Creator. In that way, no sin is more or less of an offense against the sovereign God. Additionally, there is hope for everyone who turns from any sin to the salvation found in Jesus. No individual sin is worse than another.

That being said, the particular sins of homosexuality and transsexuality are a rifle shot aimed at the heart of the family as God established it in creation. The institution of family is the first institution in all creation, so it is important to demonstrate that these sins are nothing to be trifled with or glossed over.

That being the case, the Apostle Paul warns that those who practice sexual immorality are without excuse:

> *For although they knew God, they did not glorify him as God or give him thanks, but they became futile in their thoughts and their senseless hearts were darkened. Although they claimed to be wise, they became fools and exchanged the glory of the immortal God for an image resembling mortal human beings or birds or four-footed animals or reptiles.*
>
> *Therefore God gave them over in the desires of their hearts to impurity, to dishonor their bodies among themselves. They exchanged the truth of God for a lie and worshiped and served the creation rather than the Creator, who is blessed forever! Amen.*
>
> *For this reason God gave them over to dishonorable passions. For their women exchanged the natural sexual relations for unnatural ones, and likewise the men also abandoned natural relations with women and were inflamed in their passions for one another. Men committed shameless acts with men and received in themselves the due penalty for their error.*
>
> *Romans 1:21*

As the Apostle Paul states, their sexual sin exchanged the worship of the Creator for the worship of the creature. In fact, Dr. John Piper explains that the root of homosexuality is idolatry of one's self.[37] It is worship of one's self. Rather than existing in interdependence on someone of the opposite sex, those people practicing homosexuality worship themselves by centering their affections on someone who looks like them, acts like them, thinks like them, and is even gratified like them. Instead of complementing one another and providing the balance intended by God, they set their affections ultimately on themselves.

Homosexuality is isolated as the sin that brought judgment on Sodom and Gomorrah in the time of Abraham. Inasmuch as Abraham is an example of faith and marriage, the twin cities of Sodom and Gomorrah are a blemish on that created order.

The Apostle Paul teaches that homosexuality is unnatural even though every type of sexual sin is a corruption of God's created design. Fornication, adultery, and polygamy are a corruption of God's created design through excess. Homosexuality is a corruption of God's created design by nature. The call for radical interdependence in marriage is a clarion call for created design.

Another Visit from Pagan Philosophy

Previously, we noted how a contemporary myopic view of missions insists on "professional" Christian workers. This dualism is traced back to the influence of pagan Greek philosophers through Augustine and other early church fathers. They carried on the Two-Story approach of Plato, with the Upper Story being the pure, desired world of thought, spirituality, and contem-

37 John Piper, "Why Is Homosexuality Wrong?," Desiring God, accessed April 29, 2019, https://www.desiringgod.org/interviews/why-is-homosexuality-wrong.

plation. The Lower Story is the material world and everything relating to it, such as manual labor, hunger, and sex.

Paradoxically, the lust for sexual perversions is a symptom of this same pagan Two-Story philosophy. Those practicing these sins would have us believe that the choices of their mind are more important than the dictates of their bodies. In these unnatural desires and sins, people believe that they are simply born this way which justifies them, so they are moving to make their sexual proclivities a civil right.

Francis Collins is the director of the Human Genome Project and America's most prominent geneticist. Regarding the idea that people are born with these proclivities, Collins writes, "Sexual orientation is genetically influenced but not hardwired by DNA, and...whatever genes are involved represent predispositions, not predeterminations."[38] Sexual orientation is clearly a choice. Biological sex is not a choice but rather is an indication of the material world of flesh and blood that we live in.

Practicing any sexual immorality is a mental choice of the Upper Story that elevates the mind over and above the body, which is part of the Lower Story. This choice is not a recognition, respect, and love for the created design of the Lower Story. Such a choice reflects a disdain and hatred of the mandates of their bodies, their own biology. It reflects a love of their independent mental choice of their exercise of sexuality. "Gay activists downplay the body—our biological identity as male or female—and define our true selves by our feelings and desires."[39]

---

38 Francis S. Collins, *The Language of God: A Scientist Presents Evidence for Belief* (New York, NY: Simon & Schuster, 2006), 260.

39 Nancy Pearcey, *Love Thy Body: Answering Hard Questions about Life and Sexuality* (Grand Rapids, MI: Baker Books, 2019), 223.

Consider the words to this effect from Melinda Selmys, a former lesbian,

> *Under all the hype about sex as fun and games is actually a fundamental despair. Beneath all the pageantry of free sex and self-love, there is a fundamental belief that the body doesn't mean anything, that it is insignificant in a literal sense: signifying nothing. You can do anything that you like with it. You can pleasure it with a vacuum cleaner or...you can give it away to anyone for any reason. It's just a sort of wet machine, a tool that you can use and exchange for whatever purpose suits your fancy.*[40]

Neo-Platonist pagan philosophy is so subtle as to have crept into our society's view of sexuality. It has contributed to the compartmentalization of what we do with our bodies so that we live shattered lives rather than living as whole people reflecting the image of God through our created design.

A Diamond in the Rough

The most infamous example of homosexuality in the Bible is undoubtedly the unrestrained practice of homosexuality in the cities of Sodom and Gomorrah. It is from the name of the first of these cities that the term "sodomy" was coined to identify the aberrant perversion that the men of this city engaged in. To get to this notorious story in Genesis, fast forward from Creation through the advent of sin, the curses for sin, the sinful intention of the human heart, Noah's ark to escape a world of sin, the catalog of nations, the tower of Babel and its basis in sin, and finally to the introduction of Abram in Genesis 12. Remarkably,

40 Ibid., 166.

it is here in the grand plan of God's blessing for all nations that the story of Sodom and Gomorrah's sin is recorded. In fact, this story continues Moses' pattern from the creation story forward; namely, sin followed by blessing followed by sin followed by blessing, and so forth.

We first find the blessing and inherent goodness of creation followed by corruption. With that corruption, Moses summarizes,

> *But the Lord saw that the wickedness of humankind had become great on the earth. Every inclination of the thoughts of their minds was only evil all the time.*
>
> *Genesis 6:5*

In response, the Lord brings about Noah's flood but graciously preserves humanity through the family of Noah. Even so, humankind obeys the corruption of sinful nature, and they as a group mount a direct rebellion against God in the construction of the tower of Babel, as elaborated in Chapter 10. God's response is forcible confusion of languages followed by forcible obedience to his command to be fruitful, multiply, and fill the earth. It is with this forcible scattering of people across the face of the earth that God unveils his plan of blessing all of those families having just been scattered, and once again, we see the pattern of human sin over and against God's blessing.

Following this, Abram is blessed by God to be a blessing to all nations. This point will be revisited several times throughout this book, but in this specific case, the blessing of Abram is seen in contrast to the wickedness of the people of Sodom and Gomorrah. The backdrop is set through the evil inclination of man's heart in Genesis 6 and Noah's flood through Genesis 7–10 and the Tower of Babel in Genesis 11, and Sodom and Gomorrah in Genesis 13–19. It is in this context of evil that Abram's story is shared with the rich promise of building a nation through the miraculous birth of a son.

This covenant with God is first given to Abram in Genesis 12:1–3,

> *Now the Lord said to Abram,*
>
> *"Go out from your country, your relatives, and your father's household*
>
> *to the land that I will show you.*
>
> *Then I will make you into a great nation, and I will bless you,*
>
> *and I will make your name great,*
>
> *so that you will exemplify divine blessing.*
>
> *I will bless those who bless you,*
>
> *but the one who treats you lightly I must curse,*
>
> *so that all the families of the earth may receive blessing through you."*

Abram is clearly blessed to be a blessing to all the families of the earth. This is confirmed in Genesis 17:1–4 with the promise of the birth of Isaac:

When Abram was 99 years old, the Lord appeared to him and said, "I am the Sovereign God. Walk before me and be blameless. Then I will confirm my covenant between me and you, and I will give you a multitude of descendants."

Abram bowed down with his face to the ground, and God said to him, "As for me, this is my covenant with you: You will be the father of a multitude of nations."

The promise of Isaac leads us through the change of Abram's name to Abraham and into the first verses of Genesis 18. It is followed by the last half of this chapter which introduces the blatant sin of the people of Sodom and Gomorrah. Like a diamond in the rough, this beautiful promise is reiterated once again to Abram. Right in the middle of the terrible outcry of the innocents against the people of Sodom and Gomorrah, the Lord repeats his covenant to Abraham and gives a purpose statement for his blessing,

Then the Lord said, "Should I hide from Abraham what I am about to do? After all, Abraham will surely become a great and powerful nation, and all the nations on the earth may receive blessing through him. I have chosen him so that he may command his children and his household after him to keep the way of the Lord by doing what is right and just. Then the Lord will give to Abraham what he promised him."

So the Lord said, "The outcry against Sodom and Gomorrah is so great and their sin so blatant that I must go down and see if they are as wicked as the outcry suggests. If not, I want to know."

Genesis 18:17–21

The evil deeds of Sodom and Gomorrah are a disjointed break in the natural story of Abraham. Abraham's story starts before the scene in Sodom and ends after the scene in Sodom. Other than the fact of Abraham's relative, Lot, living among the people of Sodom, we are left to wonder, why are these sinful people highlighted and given such a prominent place in the story Moses is recounting? Presumably, this is because every thought and intention of humankind was evil, as we've already seen. The sinful act of sodomy certainly would have existed in other cities in the world. Why, then, were Sodom and Gomorrah singled out as they are in this story from Scripture? After all, the story of Babel had a greater impact on the families of the earth with farther-reaching consequences. Why was Babel not given more "airtime," and why were such sinful places as Sodom and Gomorrah even mentioned considering their base immorality?

We needn't wonder too long before the answer is given to us by Moses within the story itself, "*I have chosen him so that he may command his children and his household after him to keep the way of the Lord by doing what is right and just*" (Genesis 18:19).

The reason is not to put on display the wickedness of Sodom but to make an exhibition of the righteousness of Abraham and the way of God. Abraham's life stood in stark opposition to the unrighteous and aberrant behavior of these two cities. The commandments that the Lord gave Abraham that he was to teach his children showed a completely different lifestyle than the chaotic abandonment of God's way that we see in Sodom and Gomorrah.

In Abraham, we have an example of a life walked with God. In Abraham, we have an understanding of justice and righteousness that he was to exhibit and that all of humankind was to follow. In Abraham and his wife Sarah, we have God's promise fulfilled through the interdependence of marriage. In Sodom, we have an example of utter depravity and sinful chaos untethered to truth and undeterred by any moral compass. As Christopher Wright posits in his book *The Mission of God's People*, the purpose of the story of Sodom and Gomorrah is to contrast righteous Abraham with the unrighteousness of these cities. In the godless lives of the people of Sodom and Gomorrah, we see society degenerate into the deviant behavior of sodomy.

Homosexuality is a biological dead-end street. Homosexuality cannot lead to people being fruitful and multiplying and filling the earth. Homosexuality cannot lead to the expression of the image of God as it is set out in Genesis 1 and 2.

Eros Expressed

C.S. Lewis spent most of his life as an atheist. His younger years involved sexual carousing that he strongly turned away from at thirty-three when he committed his life to the Lord.

Lewis' publishing career expressed rich theology through rigorous dialectic and imaginative and artistic fiction. Bill and Joy Gresham became avid fans of this Oxford don from their home in New York. However, their marriage unraveled because of Bill's abusive behavior as an alcoholic and serial adulterer.[41]

41 Gina Dalfonzo, "C. S. Lewis's Joy in Marriage," ChristianityToday.com (Christianity Today, October 8, 2013), https://www.christianitytoday.com/ct/2013/october-web-only/cs-lewis-joy-in-marriage.html.

Joy sought counsel from C.S. Lewis by letter and eventually moved to England to meet him in person. While in England, Bill wrote her that he had fallen in love with her cousin and divorced her. Lewis helped her financially as he often did with his friends and even married her in a civil ceremony to help her stay in England permanently. Even though this marriage was to help her immigrate, the two fell in love and were married in a religious ceremony a year later.[42]

The marriage of Joy Davidman and C.S. Lewis is described as intensely happy and satisfying even though it was cut short by Joy's cancer and death only three years later. Nonetheless, it influenced the writings of Lewis deeply by giving him a first-hand understanding of Christian marriage. In *The Four Loves*, Lewis describes Eros, this marital love,

> *There may be those who have first felt mere sexual appetite for a woman and then gone on at a later stage to "fall in love with her." But I doubt if this is at all common. Very often what comes first is simply a delighted pre-occupation with the Beloved—a general, unspecified pre-occupation with her in her totality. A man in this state really hasn't leisure to think of sex. He is too busy thinking of a person. The fact that she is a woman is far less important than the fact that she is herself. He is full of desire, but the desire many not be sexually toned. If you asked him what he wanted, the true reply would often be, "To go on thinking of her." He is love's contemplative.*[43]

42 Lyle W. Dorsett, ed., *The Essential C.S. Lewis* (New York, NY: Collier, 1988), xv.
43 Clive Staples Lewis, *The Four Loves* (San Francisco, CA: HarperCollins, 2017), 96-97.

Biblical love between a husband and wife is a complementary love designed so that each person completes what is lacking in the other. Together, their union makes a whole, integral marriage.

Even sexual union between a husband and a wife is the means God himself commissioned to express his image throughout all the world. God's covenant to Abraham is to bless many nations through his descendants produced through his marriage to Sarah. In this, we see the order and righteousness of a life dedicated to God. As another example, Pearcey notes,

> *The picture of ultimate origins given in the Bible is not one of disconnected solitary individuals wandering under the trees in a state of nature. Instead, the picture is one of a couple—male and female—related from the beginning in the social institution of marriage, forming the foundation of social life.*

> *The implication of the doctrine of the Trinity is that relationships are just as ultimate or real as individuals...Relationships are part of the created order and thus are ontologically real and good.*[44]

The marriage of Abraham and Sarah, then, is given in contrast to both the rebellion immediately preceding his story at Babel, and his marriage is given in contrast to the chaotic depravity of Sodom and Gomorrah. Before Abraham's story is introduced,

---

44 Nancy Pearcey, *Total Truth: Liberating Christianity from Its Cultural Captivity* (Wheaton, IL: Crossway Books, 2008), 138.

the contrast is a people who defiantly aim to make a name for themselves and take the seat of God himself. In the middle of Abraham's story, the contrast is a people who worship themselves as though they were God through rampant homosexuality. However, in the interdependence of Abraham and Sarah's marriage, we have a promise of blessing not only for Abraham but for all people. Their proper, moral sexual union resulted in fruitful multiplication that became a blessing to all the world.

Through Abraham's life and his example of justice and righteousness, the principle of interdependence within marriage is clear. Husbands and wives complement one another. They complete one another. They are, together, made in the image of God, and God's intent for their reproduction is tautologous to their male and female biology.

CHAPTER 10–FAMILY

#InItTogether

Some years ago, Matthew McConaughey starred in the movie *Failure to Launch,* where he plays a thirty-five-year-old man who lives in his parents' home and shows no interest in leaving the comfort of home-cooked meals and care. His parents take pains to try to push him "out of the nest," to no avail. His character is certainly not pulling his own weight in the family but rather is simply mooching off of the generosity of his parents.

Contrast that story-line with the true story of my friend Abdullah al-Dhakheel from Bahrain. Abdullah's father owned a home and a convenience store in their neighborhood. As Abdullah and his brothers grew older, they began to take more and more responsibility at the convenience store, and eventually, they ran the store as their aging father stayed home.

Abdullah and I were in our late 20s at the time, so it gave me an understanding of the family structure when Abdullah invited me to his home, and I learned that it was his father's home. Perhaps some people would have seen this as a *Failure to Launch*. I gained an even greater understanding of the family structure some years later when I visited again, and he was still living at his father's home; only this time, he was living there with his wife and two children. The family had made accommodations by building a second floor to serve as two apartments, one for his family and one for his brother's. Then, as yet another brother came of age and needed a home, they built a third floor to bring in another family to the home. Again, this might seem like a *Failure to Launch* for each of the sons who simply hadn't left their paternal home, but for me, it illustrated the sort of interdependence that I see in the book of Genesis.

Consider how the different al-Dhakheel families relied on one another and supported one another. "Rent" was on an extremely reasonable cost basis. The parents were not gouging from their children the way many rental properties gouge from people in the West. The parents, aunts, and uncles provided free childcare to each other because this is simply what was needed. As the parents aged, they did not require a retirement plan because their home was paid for, and their needs were supplied by their children, who were running the convenience store and contributing to their needs. As the parents aged greatly and could not care for themselves, there was no need for extremely expensive nursing home care—multiple families were on-hand to care for them.

This sort of interdependence on one another within a family unit demonstrates shared care for each other and shared love within a family. Even without this particular cultural model, however, it is clear to see how the different roles of family members can contribute to the well-being of all of the family members.

Standing Firm for the Family

Before diving deep into the structure and interdependence of family, I want to share a few words with those who, for one reason or another, do not live in an ideal family. It could be that you have experienced abuse or divorce or raising children as a single parent or longing to produce children of your own, but the Lord simply has not provided them. In all of these circumstances, you have the opportunity to be the strongest advocates for the way family was intended to be. If you had an abusive father, for example, you know deeper than anyone the need for a father to follow the Lord's instruction and care and love for his family. If you are a woman who fell into an adulterous affair, you know better than anyone the deep scars your actions have caused yourself, your husband, your children, your parents, and so on. If you have struggled with infertility for ten years and your heart begs the Lord for the joy of having children, you know the void more acutely than anyone can teach you. If you are a single man who has followed the Lord and saved yourself for marriage, but the Lord has not led you to the woman he has saved for you, your longing is constant. If you are left raising two children on your own because of the abuse of your ex-husband, God knows the cry of your heart, and you are a testimony to the fact that something is not right in your story.

These are examples of real life. What I write in the following pages is not to diminish or disregard the pain and longing you might feel from these broken situations. Indeed, I, myself, am from a broken family where my mother was abandoned with two children to raise. That in itself set our family up for the potential of even more dysfunction. By God's grace, my sister and I have each only been married once, and together, we have been in our marriages a combined fifty-four years. To be sure, each of us knew all too well the pain of our parents' divorce, and that gave us each a desperate resolve not to allow that to happen to us. Nonetheless, all this is to say that I understand broken families. Even in the midst of that realization, I share the following that much more strongly.

Working with an Empty Stable

Cleaning a manger is a mess. There simply is no whitewashed way to describe it. Animals do their thing, and their waste has to be forked, shoveled, scraped, swept, and powdered. My grandparents had a farm where this was the perfect task for a ten or twelve-year-old boy who couldn't run a milking machine. In fact, it was an everyday chore for me, especially in the winter when the cows spent most of their days indoors. I envied the farmers who had mechanized systems to automatically scrape the waste out to waiting manure spreading wagons so that the farmer only had to drive the spreader across the fields for fertilization. For me, I didn't know that luxury.

To be honest, I bemoaned the work. I wondered, what if the manger were completely clean? What if it were *always* clean? Wouldn't that be a farm worker's dream? Scripture even raises this specter: "*Where there are no oxen, the manger is clean, but abundant crops come by the strength of the ox*" (Proverbs 14:4, ESV).

A few decades after those farm days, I was in a Bible study, and I was again bemoaning the unending chore of picking up the toys and messes of our young children. On this particular occasion, I think it was because I stepped on a knife-shaped Lego creation in the darkness of night. I mentioned how the above verse came afresh across my tongue and put me in a better state of mind. A fellow parent, Dr. Sarah Dennis, exclaimed, "That's it! That verse is mine! I needed to hear that verse, and I claim it!" Apparently, I'm not the only parent who needed to realize the value of each role in the family. Sure, Dr. Dennis recognized with me that an empty house would be nice and pretty. An empty house would be as neat and orderly as I may have left it. But an empty house wouldn't have my children. An empty house would take away one of the richest contributions to my own life.

Consider the words of Jesus about children, "See that you do not disdain one of these little ones. For I tell you that their angels in heaven always see the face of my Father in heaven" (Matthew 18:10). Or consider the words of Solomon, "Grandchildren are like a crown to the elderly, and the glory of children is their parents" (Proverbs 17:6). Or consider the beautiful words of the poet, King David,

> *Yes, sons are a gift from the Lord;*
>
> *the fruit of the womb is a reward.*
>
> *Sons born during one's youth*
>
> *are like arrows in a warrior's hand.*
>
> *How blessed is the man who fills his quiver with them.*
>
> *They will not be put to shame when they confront enemies at the city gate.*
>
> *Psalm 127:3–5*

The Apostle Paul uses the interdependence of families to explain something as intimate as our relationship with the Savior as the Church and her Bridegroom. He introduces his discussion with a summary injunction in Ephesians 5:21 that covers all of the following discussion, "*…submitting to one another out of reverence for Christ.*" It seems that Paul exercises apostolic prescience, knowing that what he is about to say will be challenging but no less crucial for biblical family units.

Although Paul then includes a rationale for his statements, consider the naked roles and commands as he lays them out:

- Wives, submit to your own husbands.

- The husband is the head of the wife.
- Husbands, love your wives, as Christ loved the church.
- Husbands should love their wives as their own bodies.
- Let the wife see that she respects her husband.
- Children, obey your parents in the Lord.
- [Children,] "honor your father and mother."
- Fathers, do not provoke your children to anger.
- [Fathers,] bring them up in the discipline and instruction of the Lord.

Now, consider that Paul was given the commission of communicating a sense of order for the family unit in opposition to a chaotic, haphazard, "do as you will" approach toward family. What we see, then, is a web of interdependency that works. If we refrain from value judgments on the individual statements, we can see a network that holds fast as a single unit. Children have responsibilities, fathers have responsibilities, wives have responsibilities, fathers have more responsibilities, wives have more responsibilities, children have more responsibilities. The web moves from role to role to role and back again because each person is interdependent on one another for the whole unit to function in its created design.

Some have attempted to dismantle this created design by relegating the whole unit to an archaic paternalistic instruction from the first century after Christ that simply doesn't work or apply to today's world. After all, how can we maintain these expectations when fifty percent of marriages end in divorce or fifty-four percent of children grow up in broken homes?[45] Paul, however, seems to feel that this interdependent model of relationships not only applies to all time but is, indeed, traced to the very beginning, the very first man and woman, "*For this reason a man will leave his father and mother and will be joined to his wife, and the two will become one flesh*" (Ephesians 5:31 quoted from Genesis 2:24). Paul further quotes Exodus 20:12 when he writes, "*Honor your father and mother,*" which is the first commandment accompanied by a promise, namely, "*that it will go well with you and that you will live a long time on the earth*" (Ephesians 6:2–3). Paul gives every indication that this is the created design of interdependency the Lord intends for all time.

That being said, it is not without contention. Of course, in an age where homosexual "husbands" and husbands or "wives" and wives are permitted to adopt and raise children, those children will not be brought up "*in the discipline and instruction of the Lord*" (Ephesians 6:4). Many governments have condoned these make-believe marriages that share nothing with the created design of our biology. Indeed, Nancy Pearcey notes, "The destruction of the family is often simply one tool for increasing government power over individuals by eliminating competing loyalties, in an attempt to create total allegiance to the state."[46] Recall the result of Jean Jacques Rousseau's philosophy that citizens would be independent of their fellow men and absolutely dependent on the state.

---

45 Dave Bohon, "Broken Homes in the United States Are at Alarming Level, Study Finds," The New American, November 23, 2011, https://www.thenewamerican.com/culture/family/item/829-broken-homes-in-the-united-states-are-at-alarming-level-study-finds.

46 Nancy Pearcey, *Total Truth: Liberating Christianity from Its Cultural Captivity* (Wheaton, IL: Crossway Books, 2008), 131.

Of course, this accusation cannot be leveled against every government. Rather, it is appropriate for governments to stand by their actions that belie their true intentions. This is obvious in the case of communist governments such as the former Soviet Union. The communist state could not tolerate allegiance to religion or allegiance to any social club or order, or even allegiance to family that detracted from the individual's allegiance to the state. This demand of absolute allegiance to the state thrives even now in the Chinese communist government.

In the case of the United States, motives may be less evident, but the aim of increasing dependence on the state is the clear direction of the government. The allegiance to a militia group, as an example, is a threat to the government's control over individuals. By the same measure, the nuclear family unit is a threat when allegiances to the family are stronger than allegiance to the state. Consequently, the erosion of the nuclear family through abortion, homosexual marriage, gender choice, etc., are initiatives that weaken the family unit and make the individual increasingly dependent on the state. Civil rights no longer become inalienable rights of birth, but they become rights of choice. The family unit is discarded in favor of the government, which grants these so-called civil rights.

Family relationships, then, are integral to life in an orderly society. Immoral definitions of family that erode interdependent, God-given relationships lead to chaos. When a choice is allowed to become a civil right, a person might choose to have a civil union with her dog, or a man might file taxes jointly with his iguana because of his endearment to the reptile. After all, "love is love."

Living an integral, whole life entails recognizing our own biology and created design. To disregard this is to tread the road to chaos. Indeed, "certain virtues necessary for spiritual maturity—

such as faithfulness and self-sacrificing love—can be practiced only within relationship."[47] As much as someone might hope, relationships with reptiles simply do not lead to an integral life.

Summary

The biblical institution of family ordained by God is that "*a man leaves his father and mother and unites with his wife, and they become one family*" (Genesis 2:24). To twist this sexual union into any other perversion of fornication, adultery, polygamy, homosexuality, bestiality, or anything else will not lead to an integral life. Yet, adhering to this created design lays the foundation for a powerful, interdependent unit—the family—which is a building block for an ordered society. This foundation lends an environment to bring children "*up in the discipline and instruction of the Lord.*" This environment allows us to reflect God's image as creators, curators, and cultivators.

47 Nancy Pearcey, *Total Truth: Liberating Christianity from Its Cultural Captivity* (Wheaton, IL: Crossway Books, 2008), 133.

CHAPTER 11–COMMUNITY

#DareToCare

> *To isolate is to die.*
> *– Recovering alcoholic*
> *Sober for eight years*

On December 31, 2019, Chinese authorities notified the World Health Organization of a novel strain of coronavirus from the interior city of Wuhan that caused upper respiratory infections and a high rate of death among those infected. By all appearances, this new coronavirus strain was projected to be as virulent as Influenza, but it carried ten times the morbidity. As the virus, which came to be known as COVID-19, spread across China and through Asia, countries with particularly high populations of elderly were deeply affected, such as Italy and Spain.

On March 11, 2020, the World Health Organization declared COVID-19 a worldwide pandemic. In response, the world embarked on the first-of-its-kind social experiment of a nearly complete shutdown of society. Commerce effectively ceased. Immigration was halted. Recreation and even the walking of dogs were severely restricted. Travel stopped so suddenly that environmentalists began to study the effect of such an abrupt pause on air pollution since the world had never seen such a massive shutdown of a population.

California was first to issue a statewide lock-down. This decision was made by Governor Gavin Newsom based on computer modeling that projected fifty-six percent of the forty million residents would be infected with the virus within eight weeks.[48] These models further projected that, with a morbidity rate of nearly two percent, this particular coronavirus was expected to kill nearly half a million people in California alone within eight weeks.

Concurrent with this lock-down, the Department of Homeland Security issued its "Memorandum on Identification of Essential Critical Infrastructure Workers During COVID-19 Response" on March 19, 2020. This guidance labeled entire industries such as "medical and healthcare, telecommunications, information technology systems, defense, food and agriculture, transportation and logistics, energy, water and wastewater, law enforcement, and public works" as "essential," whereas other industries were deemed non-essential.

At the outset, these classifications and drastic measures were accepted by most people with the understanding that we all needed to make sacrifices on behalf of the people most vulnerable to the virus. With a sense of altruism, people reluctantly accepted that they would go without paychecks for the duration of the two-week emergency effort. Along those lines, an astonishing multi-trillion-dollar handout package helped the American people with $1200 checks sent to most taxpayers whether it was needed or not.

As unprecedented as these changes were, the initial aim of the dramatic reaction of these states was to "flatten the curve," with the idea being to lengthen the infection curve so that it would stay within the threshold of the medical system to manage the number of hospitalizations. Respirators and ECMO (Extra-

48 Kathleen Ronayne, "California Governor Issues Statewide Stay-at-Home Order," WJXT (WJXT News4JAX, March 20, 2020), https://www.news4jax.com/news/local/2020/03/20/california-governor-orders-statewide-stay-at-home-order.

corporeal Membrane Oxygenation) machines became regular members of our vocabulary as seemingly everyone was an overnight social media expert on managing respiratory illness.

However, what began as an attempt to "flatten the curve" morphed into an attempt to stop the progression of COVID-19. These efforts began with the simple but painful recognition that viruses kill people until herd immunity is achieved. The restrictive measures taken were intended to manage the fateful fact that many people would die before herd immunity stabilized the effect of the virus on the population.

Unfortunately, a major change took place in the thinking of society as a whole and governments as representatives of society. People mistook these efforts to "flatten the curve" as an effort to stop COVID-19 and to prevent the virus from infecting anyone. This shift came with the expectation of the economies of the world to remain under lock-down until an effective vaccine could be developed, mass-produced, and distributed to protect the entire populace. What started as a two-week emergency action was extended by another one-month emergency action which was extended by another one-month emergency action with the possibility of an indefinite suspension of work across the globe that might last twelve to eighteen months.

Despite these draconian measures to stop the spread, coronavirus infections moved steadily forward. Two and a half months of unprecedented societal disruption did not stop the progress of coronavirus in any notable way. In fact, Stanford University biophysicist Michael Levitt, a British American Israeli who won the 2013 Nobel Prize in chemistry, stated that coronavirus lock-downs might have cost more lives than they saved. Cutting against the current of mainstream media, Levitt said, "I think lock-down saved no lives. I think it may have cost lives."[49] Levitt called the restrictive measures "a very blunt and very medieval weapon" and noted that "the epidemic could have been stopped just as effectively with other sensible measures." At the very least, the response to COVID-19 caused immeasurable damage to the world's economy, but it also eroded the fabric of our inter-woven society. In short, this response is a grim illustration of the destruction of the principles of *the integral life* and society as we know it. For years to come, we will be unraveling the effects of these restrictive measures and, perhaps, most importantly, the effect of classifying whole segments of society as non-essential.

The Vacation You Never Wanted

Many people begrudge the fact that work is necessary. The wish to be independently wealthy is a common dream so that people can spend all of their days relaxing and doing only the things they most enjoy.

After nearly three months of unpaid leave from work, it became extremely rare to hear people bemoan the necessity of daily work. Rather, during those three months, it was common to hear people verbally wish that they could get back to work. Many people continue to experience deep depression and anxiety eighteen months later, not only because of the financial fallout from the decisions of politicians but from the disconnect in relationships and the "social" distancing, which was anything but social. In his book *The 5 Love Languages*, Gary Chapman details how physical touch is one of the primary ways that many people experience

---

49 Jackie Salo, "Nobel Prize Winner: Coronavirus Lockdowns Cost Lives Instead of Saving Them," New York Post (New York Post, May 26, 2020), https://nypost.com/2020/05/26/nobel-prize-winner-coronavirus-lockdowns-saved-no-lives/amp/.

love and affection from others. In an age when a touch on the shoulder at work or a hug at church, or even a simple handshake between friends is *verboten*, we as a society suffer.

In my own family network, we experienced a funeral that was not related to coronavirus, but even close family members such as healthy grandchildren or siblings were not permitted to attend the funeral. Only ten people were permitted to attend, and they were required to refrain from touching while staying at least six feet apart. The fact of the matter is, perpetual six-foot spacing between people is not sustainable, yet that is becoming the cultural norm even as restrictions have relaxed.

This common-sense narrative is even evident to the movie, music, and film magazine *Rolling Stone* which published an article early on in the COVID-19 pandemic noting, "Coronavirus Is Wreaking Havoc On Our Mental Health."[50] *The Daily Mail* quantified the impact with the estimate that 150,000 Brits would die an "avoidable death" during the coronavirus pandemic through depression, domestic violence, and suicides.[51] While any death is grievous, it is important to note that in the eighteen months of impact from COVID-19, fewer than 130,000 have died in the U.K. from coronavirus.

Other dangers include anxiety, phobias, or sickness from other preventable causes that people forego because of fear of social interaction or restricted interaction. Dr. Dan Eichenberger, a

50 EJ Dickson, "Coronavirus Is Wreaking Havoc on Our Mental Health," Rolling Stone (Rolling Stone, March 11, 2020), https://www.rollingstone.com/culture/culture-news/coronavirus-covid-19-mental-health-crisis-961247/.

51 Vanessa Chalmers, "150,000 Brits Will Die during Coronavirus Pandemic through Domestic Violence and Suicides," Daily Mail Online (Associated Newspapers, April 10, 2020), https://www.dailymail.co.uk/news/article-8207783/150-000-Brits-die-coronavirus-pandemic-domestic-violence-suicides.html.

medical doctor and the former president of an Indiana hospital, recounts in an April 4, 2020 interview that one of his patients had an "elective" heart bypass surgery postponed because of the coronavirus restrictions. When asked what happened to that patient, Dr. Eichenberger shared, "Unfortunately, he died waiting for his 'elective' procedure."[52] One can reasonably ask how many thousands of patients like him similarly lost their lives not because of coronavirus sickness but because of the response. Postponing life-saving "elective" procedures underscores the interdependence we have on one another. This man's procedure was deemed "non-essential," yet it was critically essential to sustain his life.

The fact is that we are an integrated society where we are interdependent on one another not only for the various jobs we do, such as heart surgery, but for accountability, comfort, encouragement, affirmation, and even touch. We operate as a fully functioning society only when each of us plays the roles that God intended and enabled us to do. Heart surgery is essential, plumbing is essential, data entry is essential, nursing is essential, and banking is essential. None of us can be an expert in all things, so all of us depend on one another. We are all essential for a fully functioning society.

Leaving the World Behind

Dick Proenneke lived most of his life as a carpenter, but he had a long-standing dream to retire and live alone in the Alaskan wilderness for a full year.[53] At age fifty, he took his chance. In 1967,

52 Cross Examined, *Cross Examined* (Frank Turek, April 4, 2020), https://subsplash.com/crossexamined/media/mi/+6zyw-mjw.

53 *Alone in the Wilderness* (Bob Swerer Productions, 2003).

he embarked on his adventure of felling his own trees, hauling his own sand and gravel for a foundation, and building his own cabin. Not only did Dick Proenneke succeed in his one-year adventure, but he lived the next thirty years at his cabin alone in the wilderness.

We know of Dick Proenneke's feat because of the film documentary produced about his life, titled *Alone in the Wilderness*. What seems like an astounding marathon of individualism and isolation was, however, critically dependent on the expertise and efforts of others. Not only did Dick Proenneke spend decades mastering his carpentry skills that he learned from others, but he spent years studying, planning, and preparing for his "individualistic, isolated" adventure. He used maps and navigational tools made by others to find his wilderness homestead. He used tools forged by others' hands for every step of his building adventure. He hunted and fished with implements made by others. In fact, he was critically dependent on supply runs by airplanes that delivered his food, fuel, and so on. Dick Proenneke seems to be the ultimate thirty-year lone ranger, but in reality, he was deeply integrated into society throughout the duration of his commendable adventure.

Even though his teaching is to encourage men especially, Stephen Mansfield shares thoughts that apply to women and men alike. Mr. Mansfield relates to what we've seen in the life of Dick Proenneke, "Americans, for example, have a soft place in their hearts for the image of the solitary man on horseback who rode out into the western frontier."[54] Even so, he shares further that when he lived isolated and detached from men who supported and strengthened him, "I certainly had no one to say the tough things I needed to hear, to inspire me, to laugh with me, and

54 Stephen Mansfield, *Building Your Band of Brothers* (Pennsauken, NJ: BookBaby, 2017).

to celebrate the victories when they came."[55] So, he teaches and encourages that men should build a band of brothers. That being said, he clarifies, "A band of brothers, in the sense that we use the words in this book, is not a meeting, a club, a therapy group, or a self-help society. It is the group of men we do life with."[56] In this way, he very accurately describes *the integral life*. A whole life consists of interdependent relationships in which we "do life" with each other.

Even though the manner of relating to one another is different, women have no less of a need for these relationships in the integral life. Mansfield's description is so apt that it is worth quoting here in full:

> *I need men who know what I can be and know what might keep me from it. I need men who can push me to my destiny.*
>
> *Let me be even more specific. I need men who walk closely enough with me to notice the angry cell phone call I just had with my wife. They have to have the courage to mention it and ask what's going on. They help. They insist upon my best.*
>
> *They are also near enough to know when I'm checking out the backside of the waitress. They point it out. They challenge me. They ask what's going on at home.*

---

55 Ibid.

56 Ibid.

> *I want to walk through life with men who know that my particular problems aren't booze or women, but pride, foul language, and the twenty or thirty Oreos at a time that always seem like a good idea.*[57]

Mansfield's weakness with Oreos hits home so closely that it seems he knows me personally! In fact, he's describing normal life with the candor that we all need.[58] He's describing the interdependence on others to live the integral life.

The Lord has given me a band of brothers like Mansfield describes, but I have to admit that our lack of geographical proximity has stretched the definition a bit. My closest friend since high school has been Jon Oehmcke. It seemed to be more than chance that allowed us to fasten our hearts together, similar to David and Jonathan in the Bible. Not only do we share many similar interests, but we balance each other's interests as well. In the 1980s and 1990s, we shared a love of ultimate frisbee, music, and mechanic work. We spent inordinate hours running up and down a grassy field chasing an old pie pan, and we spent inordinate hours exploring new genres of Christian heavy metal. Being poor students, we spent even more time fixing old cars, trucks, and motorcycles.

As it happened, my path took more of an academic path through college while Jon took more of a technical path designing and building boards to control robotic machinery. Whereas I spent my career in inner-city ministry and missions, he bought a farmhouse and has lived in that home for decades.

---

57 Ibid.

58 Art of Manliness, *Art of Manliness*, January 31, 2017, https://www.artofmanliness.com/articles/podcast-274-building-band-brothers/.

Nonetheless, we served as best men in each other's weddings and continued to live out the proverb, "*Iron sharpens iron, so one man sharpens another*" (Proverbs 27:17, NASB). Our particular method of holding each other accountable came through car rides and long walks on the breakwater at the Port of Sheboygan, Wisconsin. In short, we did life together. In those times, we would be able to discern areas of weakness in character, and we showed no fear in pointing out those flaws. We were there for each other through failures and trials, as well as successes and joys. Despite taking different paths in our life pursuits, there has been no mismatch in understanding each other. In fact, those differences in our educational direction and career pursuits have made us that much more respectful of the advice and counsel we give. In short, Jon balances me and acts as a ballast to steady me in storms.

This is the integral life lived out through interdependence within the community. I would not be the same person I am today were it not for fastening my heart to Jon in 1987. I am so grateful that this deep friendship continues to strengthen me as much today as ever.

A Novel Response to a Novel Virus

This chapter began with a look at the 2020 pandemic and the damage to society that was wrought not by the virus itself but by the reaction to the virus. The massive swing to isolation undermined the fabric of society as we know it and threatened institutions far more than the economic engines that keep us busy.

Many have sought to compare this response to other pandemics, from the 1918 Spanish Flu to the Antonine Plague of A.D. 165 to the Plague of Cyprian in A.D. 251. Dr. Kathryn McKinley has undertaken to compare the response of society to that of the Bubonic Plague of 1348 in her article *How the Rich Reacted to the*

Bubonic Plague Has Eerie Similarities to Today's Pandemic. With unimaginable virulence, the plague killed forty to fifty percent of the population of Europe. Those infected went from healthy to the grave within four to seven days. Dr. McKinley points out the relevance of this response to today's pandemic by summarizing a book by Boccaccio that recounts one hundred stories of middle-class merchants and servants in *The Decameron.* Dr. McKinley describes,

> *...the rich secluding themselves at home, where they enjoy quality wines and provisions, music and other entertainment. The very wealthiest—whom Boccaccio describes as "ruthless" —deserted their neighborhoods altogether, retreating to comfortable estates in the countryside, "as though the plague was meant to harry only those remaining within their city walls."*[59]

The wealthy had the means to isolate. Their choice was to withdraw from society rather than participate in it. In the 2020 panic, the state forced isolation by fiat, which had devastating effects on the sense of community. Of course, the means of funding this unprecedented shutdown is through trillions of dollars of debt that will cripple the day-to-day economy of future generations that are saddled with the debt.

Even for us, it is dangerous to overlook the relationship that ordinary citizens now have with the state after these handouts. Nancy Pearcey wrote the following long before this pandemic,

59 Kathryn McKinley, "How the Rich Reacted to the Bubonic Plague Has Eerie Similarities to Today's Pandemic," The Conversation, April 25, 2021, https://theconversation.com/how-the-rich-reacted-to-the-bubonic-plague-has-eerie-similarities-to-todays-pandemic-135925.

but the warning is all the more apropos,

> *It may seem paradoxical that a philosophy of radical individualism would lead to radical statism. But as Hannah Arendt points out in The Origins of Totalitarianism, disconnected, isolated individuals are actually the most vulnerable to totalitarian control because they have no competing identity or loyalties. That's why one of the best ways to protect individual rights is by protecting the rights of groups such as families, churches, schools, businesses, and voluntary associations. Strong, independent social groupings actually help to limit the state because each claims its own sphere of responsibility and jurisdiction, thus preventing the state from controlling every aspect of life. Neo-Calvinist political philosophy describes the independence of social spheres using the term sphere sovereignty, meaning the right of each to its own limited jurisdiction over against the other spheres.*[60]

The dangers of becoming dependent on the state include totalitarianism, communism, and fascism, all of which have been proven heinous enemies of culture by history. Eroding normal societal function of interdependent individuals will shape our world like no other social experiment.

---

60 Nancy Pearcey, *Total Truth: Liberating Christianity from Its Cultural Captivity* (Wheaton, IL: Crossway Books, 2008), 141.

Conclusion

A healthy society is comprised of individuals fully contributing to society with all of their various gifts and fields of knowledge. We are not a mere association of lone rangers. We are a cooperative operating in a community by God's created design. This is the interdependence described in the integral life. It is in living out the integral life that we fulfill our mission to be fruitful, multiply, fill the earth, work it, and keep it.

CHAPTER 12–CHURCH

#ChurchBodyBuilders

One of the advantages I have had as both a pastor and the president of a mission agency is that of interacting with people on the "home front" and those going into cross-cultural missions. Recently in my role as pastor, I offended a teenage girl in one of my sermons. In fact, she walked out of the room right at that moment.

After the service, I had an opportunity to ask her father about what I had shared. He heard the sermon and wasn't alarmed by what I said. He perceived the teaching as soundly biblical. In fact, he noted that it sounded to him like it was an open opportunity to talk with his daughter about this important issue.

An unrelated woman in the church immediately left the sermon as well and went to be with that young girl. I wrote to her later that day,

> *Even though we are open to [everyone] and we aim to present a loving environment, the message of the church doesn't change. The only way for people to find the hope of salvation from sin is to recognize sin, repent from it, and find forgiveness in Jesus. That is the most loving thing we can share. We absolutely want to provide that sort of loving environment where people will be accepted while the truth is proclaimed nonetheless.*

In fact, I would say that you offered just that, today. Each person in the church provides gifts that support people as a whole. On the one hand, I believe I proclaimed the truth of the Bible, which evidently did offend. On the other hand, you provided the support and assurance of acceptance... Both of us served purposes in the church that support the needs of people to hear the truth while also being accepted.

This woman acted as a check and balance for the care of this girl. Secondly, she and I had a respectful interchange. Finally, the Church was better because of the roles each of us played in this instance, and we were affirmed that these roles were appropriate and right.

Had it been me alone, I might have offended this young woman and turned her off to the teaching of the Church as a whole. However, this woman provided something I couldn't. I was dependent on her to fulfill her role in the Church, and she was dependent on me to fulfill my role in the Church. We are better together in the interdependence of the Integral Life.

Fundamentalist Roots

In the interest of full disclosure, I have to admit my own tendency to isolationism and fundamentalism in the Church. I recognize that I had this tendency from my teenage years when I saw things through a very black and white lens, but I think I built this tendency through my college years at the University of Northwestern—St. Paul by adding more and more knowledge. Now, make no mistake; I love my *alma mater,* and I am grateful for the thorough biblical training that I continue to use every day. Nonetheless, the school had its start as a fundamentalist missionary and Bible training school and holds its place in history as one of the three foremost fundamentalist schools of the first half of the 1900s, alongside Moody Bible Institute and the Bible Institute of Los Angeles (BIOLA).

The important element of fundamentalism to recognize is that it is based in degrees of separation. For example, Christians live a life different from the world, which separates them from what the world does. This is first-degree separation.

Second-degree separation is refraining from association with people who think, act like, and do the things of the world. "Don't drink, don't smoke, don't chew, don't go with girls who do" is a humorous mantra that describes second-degree separation.

Third-degree separation is refraining from association with people who associate with people who think, act like, and do the things of the world. This level of separation sounds ridiculous to some, but a notable recipient of this separation was the great evangelist Billy Graham. Because Billy Graham would not distance himself from ecumenical denominations or liberal politicians, he was excluded from fellowship from some of his earlier associations in his fundamentalist roots.

The piece that I find so painful in this is the realization of lost opportunity in making Christ known throughout the world. Because many in the Church have walked the path of *separation* and *isolation*, I can't help but imagine the potential power of the Church that has been lost by the lack of interdependence. Fortunately for me, the University of Northwestern—St. Paul had long since made the shift to Evangelicalism in place of Fundamentalism by the time I attended there, but the tendency to mark lines that divide was strong in me as a person, irrespective of the position of the college when I studied.

Body Builders

When I first started my work in missions, I attended a workshop put on by The Body Builders that taught the basics of raising personal support. The instructor, Steve Shadrach, had to give a disclaimer when he introduced the organization, however, because a number of people from previous workshops had gone online to look up The Body Builders and landed on web pages filled with scantily clad men and women able to lift a Toyota with a single hand! Perhaps it wasn't that extreme, but the caution was needed to ensure that people made it to the right website of The Body Builders.

The Apostle Paul introduces the analogy of the Body of Christ and the Church. He revisits this analogy repeatedly and expands it to become one of his favorite descriptions of the Church. In fact, when speaking of the Church as a body and people as members of the body, it's interesting to note that our term for "member" of any group of people is derived from Paul's use of "members." Mark the irony when you hear of the "membership" of atheist organizations!

The members of the Body of Christ are the indispensable arms, legs, etc., that make up the whole. To be candid, I can't improve on Paul's words himself. It only makes sense to explore a few of the many passages calling the Church the Body of Christ.

> *For just as in one body we have many members, and not all the members serve the same function, so we who are many are one body in Christ, and individually we are members who belong to one another. And we have different gifts according to the grace given to us. If the gift is prophecy, that individual must use it in proportion to his faith. If it is service, he must serve; if it is teaching, he*

must teach; if it is exhortation, he must exhort; if it is contributing, he must do so with sincerity; if it is leadership, he must do so with diligence; if it is showing mercy, he must do so with cheerfulness.

Romans 12:4–8

There are several points to be drawn from this passage. The first is that all the members of the Church are necessary. The whole ministry of the Church cannot be done without the representation of all the various gifts distributed according to the Spirit's will.

Second, each person is dependent on the gifts of the other. Teachers are dependent on those who give to the Church generously. Teachers may not have the means to give to the level that a business owner might. I know many teachers who would say "Yes!" and "Amen!" to that. On the other hand, those same business owners might not have the patience to corral a dozen five-year-olds and deliver an effective Bible lesson. I know many business owners who would say "Yes!" and "Amen!" to that. We are interdependent on each other to fulfill all the functions God intended for his Church, his Body.

Perhaps the most well-known teaching of Paul on the Body of Christ is in 1 Corinthians 12:12–30, which is quoted here as a unit because the logic is so tightly knit:

For just as the body is one and yet has many members, and all the members of the body—though many—are one body, so too is Christ. For in one Spirit we were all baptized into one body. Whether Jews or Greeks or slaves or free, we were all made to drink of the one Spirit. For in fact the body is not a single member, but many. If the foot says, "Since I am not a hand, I am not part of the body," it does not lose its membership in the body because of that. And if the ear says, "Since I am not an eye, I am not part of the body," it does not lose its membership in the body because of that. If the whole body were an eye, what part would do the hearing? If the whole were an ear, what part would exercise the sense of smell? But as a matter of fact, God has placed each of the members in the body just as he decided. If they were all the same member, where would the body be? So now there are many members, but one body. The eye cannot say to the hand, "I do not need you," nor in turn can the head say to the foot, "I do not need you." On the contrary, those members that seem to be weaker are essential, and those members we consider less honorable we clothe with greater honor, and our unpresentable members are clothed with dignity, but our presentable members do not need this. Instead, God has blended together the body, giving greater honor to the lesser member, so that there may be no division in the body, but the members may have mutual concern for one another. If one member suffers, everyone suffers with it. If a member is honored, all rejoice with it.

Now you are Christ's body, and each of you is a member of it. And God has placed in the church first apostles, second prophets, third teachers, then miracles, gifts of healing, helps, gifts of leadership, different kinds of tongues. Not all are

> *apostles, are they? Not all are prophets, are they? Not all are teachers, are they? Not all perform miracles, do they? Not all have gifts of healing, do they? Not all speak in tongues, do they? Not all interpret, do they?*

Paul builds on the analogy of a body to illustrate how ridiculous it is for people to desire to be what they are not. For instance, some attribute to Shakespeare the phrase, "The eyes are the window to the soul." The eyes are so prominent in our social engagement and connectedness. Yet, the eye cannot dispense with the rest of the body, and the rest of the body cannot become all eyes. As prominent as eyes are, there are only two in each person.

Paul uses the plain, laughable humor of this suggestion to point out that the members of the Church cannot all be one type. It does not matter if the gift of that member is as prominent as speaking in tongues or as hidden as administration. Not everyone can be just one member of the Body. Just as not every member of the body can be a left big toe, not every member of the church can be responsible for prophecy, for example. For the whole function of the integral life of the Church, all the gifts that the Spirit distributes must be encouraged, appreciated, and fostered.

Seeing What's Not There

Many people struggle to see what's not there. It sounds obvious, doesn't it? Yet, the question is legitimate; how can we quantify the impact of something that is not there? For instance, if I share with you that sixty-one million babies have been terminated by abortion in the US since the procedure was legalized, you should be asking what the impact has been for society. Those babies are absent. What would their contribution have been?

Supreme Court Justice Ruth Bader Ginsburg voiced in 2009, "Frankly, I had thought that at the time Roe was decided, there was concern about population growth and particularly growth in populations that we don't want to have too many of. So that Roe was going to be then set up for Medicaid funding for abortion."[61] Justice Ginsburg expressed, then, that she supported abortion because it was a means of eugenics, that is, eliminating undesirables from the populace. Presumably, Justice Ginsburg wasn't seeing her own Caucasian demographic as those "we don't want to have too many of," but even if black, Latino, and Asian minorities were those "we don't want to have too many of," what is the impact on society? Of those sixty-one million lives that have been terminated, what inventions or creations or discoveries have been lost? Was the cure for cancer in one of Justice Ginsburg's undesirables? Was the vaccine for last chapter's COVID-19 in the mind of one of the children that "we don't want to have too many of"? Indeed, were future Supreme Court justices terminated as merely undesirables? How many justices and politicians and inventors and scientists and economists and electricians and manufacturers and educators have we terminated? It really is hard to quantify the impact on society when we recognize that each of us plays such a significant role. We are interdependent on one another, but our society is falling short in so many places. One reason is certainly because these pieces of society are missing.

The same point could be made of the Church. In each matter that we see a weakness or failure or fault in the Church today, we shouldn't just ask *what is missing*, but *who is missing*? God has equipped the Church with all of the gifts to accomplish all

61 Emily Bazelon, "The Place of Women on the Court," The New York Times (The New York Times, July 7, 2009), https://www.nytimes.com/2009/07/12/magazine/12ginsburg-t.html.

it will do. Do we see an area of need where the Church plays no relevant part? For example, is the Church playing a relevant part in setting sex trafficking victims free? Is the Church playing a relevant part in preventing nuclear war with Russia? Is the Church even accomplishing the religious commission to reach the Unreached People Groups of the earth?

In each of these problem areas, there are people who have been given gifts by the Holy Spirit who are not using them. That results in a chain reaction of people who are not even believers who fail to realize that they have gifts they are not using. They haven't identified their gifts because they haven't identified the Savior.

To make this clearer, consider my fictitious friend, John. John runs a thriving Internet business, so he is doing quite well. However, he has never been introduced to the concept of using his gift of generosity, so he faithfully puts $20 into the offering plate each week when his $250,000 annual earnings would easily allow him to give $2000 per week. Not only is John robbed of the joy of using his gift and giving cheerfully, but another church member, Kim, is robbed of the funds necessary to send her to China as an English teacher so that she can use her gifts of evangelism. Because Kim has been raising support for years, her vision is withering, and Xian in Beijing has not heard the Gospel. Because Xian has not heard the Gospel, he hasn't shared it with his sister, Changying, who has no future hope. Subsequently, she begins working in the sex industry in Shanghai.

This fictitious chain reaction could go on *ad infinitum* because the fact is, we are failing as the Church to fulfill our gifts and do what we are gifted to do. It is only when we break out of the myopic view of "missions" and begin to live the integral life that we will see complete passion and purpose for God lived out through the Church.

Summary

The Church is the institution God has commissioned for global change. The Church is the institution commissioned with caring for his Bride and ministering to the world. The Church is commissioned to preach the Good News to all people everywhere.

The functions of the Church are so tightly integrated that they are comparable to the indispensable members of a body. Like a body, the function is missing if one of its members is absent. When we see the needs and problems of the world being unmet, it is an indicator that the members of the Church that God has equipped to do the work have disregarded their role. It is only when all of the interdependent functions of the Church are being accomplished that we will know the integral life for the Church, the Body of Christ.

SECTION 3–TO THE ENDS OF THE EARTH

Zealot. That could have been my nickname, to be sure. My life was revolutionized by Jesus. It was turned downside up. What I had minimized—responsibility, obedience, and faith—now dictated my actions and thoughts and words. My life was upended by reading the Bible daily. One hour, two hours, four hours, five hours. This saturation in the Word washed my mind of its foul language, devious thinking, vandalism, and images of pornography that I had indulged in. The Bible drove these things from my life like a pheasant being flushed from its nest by a bloodthirsty hound. Almost overnight, my life took on new meaning, real purpose, and aim because of the Bible.

The Bible was the undeniable influence at work in my life. Even so, many people were involved in this radical transformation. I think of my mother's faith being my starting point as a child. It was her faith that got me to church so that I heard the dangers of hell during Sunday School. In fact, my Sunday School teacher was reticent to share the lesson of hell that day. She noted that many people feel that hell shouldn't be spoken of to children only nine years old. Nonetheless, she taught us about the risk of everlasting torment apart from God. She taught us that there was just one thing that separated those going to hell from those going to heaven, namely, faith in Jesus to forgive our sins. I didn't "pray the prayer" that day, but I did take note of it.

Later that week, while walking home from school, I stopped and quietly talked to God, saying, "God, I'm not sure if I've said this before, but I want you to know that I believe in Jesus, and I ask you to take the punishment for all of my sins. In Jesus' name, Amen." And there I had it. Fire insurance to keep me from hell.

From that point, I generally continued to do what I wanted, and my life spiraled downward into depression, suicidal thoughts, pornography, swearing at my teachers, smoking, fighting, vandalism, theft, and many other steps far from the path my "fire insurance" should have paved for me. This pattern of living went on for the next six years until I stopped in exasperation as a teenager, "There must be something more to life! Here I am wasting five days of the week just to get to the adrenalin high of the two days of weekend parties. There must be something more to life!"

This simple realization started a quest for something to fill the void in life. I had tried many sports and activities like football, basketball, wrestling, and chess. I was looking for camaraderie and purpose, but I kept coming up short.

As it would happen, I turned to our free community newspaper, *The Action Advertiser*, to find something to give my life purpose. There I found a small advertisement for Campus Life, a high-energy youth group that met every Tuesday at 7:29 PM. Thinking that this was a formal sort of group, I put on a collared shirt and tie and showed up half an hour early to make a good impression. Of course, the group consisted of high school students, not businessmen, so I quickly found that I was the *only* student who showed up in a collared shirt and tie and the *only* student who showed up half an hour early. Even so, a college-age volunteer named Ron Riemersma came out of a backroom where other volunteers had gathered, and he hung out with me until other students started to arrive. As they started to file in, the volunteers and staff came out of that back room where, as I learned later, they had been praying for the evening's meeting and the impact it could have on students. No one made fun of me for over-dressing or arriving so early. Instead, I found a welcoming group of high school students that participated in crazy games, energetic discussions, and serious teaching about normal things that every teenager deals with. I had found a new home.

I didn't know it at the time, but Campus Life was a high school ministry of Youth for Christ. In an appealing, non-confronting way, the staff taught us to ground ourselves in life through faith in Jesus. We weren't "Bible-beaten." That is, the Bible wasn't crammed down our throats, but it was taught as the answer to life's greatest questions and problems.

At this point, I would say that I was drawn into Campus Life by the people. I was drawn in by the care that Ron showed me and Janelle Bruins and Bill Olmstead and Linda Vande Zande. As staff and volunteers, they helped to guide me and steer me toward the Savior. I was beginning to see the pieces of a committed life.

The staff drew me in, but my new friends kept me there. Many of them are fast friends to this day, and without them, I wouldn't have gotten to the Bible the way I did. It was the warmth of all of these people that kept me coming so that when the doors of the Campus Life building were open, I was there. For nine months, I scarcely missed a meeting, and after that time, I was invited to be a student leader. However, that role had a number of responsibilities that I had to agree to:

- I had to attend three out of four Campus Life meetings each month.
- I had to attend all of the student leader meetings.
- I had to attend church three out of four weeks each month.
- I had to read my Bible for half an hour each day.

At first, I balked at this list of commitments. Sure, I could attend the Campus Life meetings, and I could attend the Student Leader meetings because I was already in the building every time I could be. On the other hand, I wasn't part of a church, so I hesitated at that. Also, I felt I was too busy to commit to thirty minutes a day of Bible reading. So, I sat on the decision through the summer when I joined the Campus Life group attending DC '88, a Youth Congress on Evangelism.

While at DC '88, I heard powerful motivational talks from speakers like Josh McDowell and Buster Soaries and even President and Nancy Reagan. By the end of the conference, I had made the decision to be a student leader, and my life took a hard swing toward direct evangelism.

Still, I wasn't reading my Bible, and candidly, this was a process for me, but this was the absolutely crucial ingredient that transformed my life. At first, I started out reading only about ten minutes each day, then fifteen, then I finally got to the required thirty minutes per day. Around this time, I wrote from Wisconsin to California to a pastor who had been prayerfully watching over our family since we had attended his church for one year when I was seven years old. He continued this care of watching over our family with prayer for eight years. After those years that C.W. Walberg was praying for us, he was overjoyed when I told him that I had rededicated my life to the Lord. In fact, he sent me a library of about seventy books, including a leather-bound Bible, commentaries, Bible encyclopedias, Christian biographies, and on and on. I am still using many of those books today that he sent to me thirty years ago, but at that time, I dove headfirst into studying the Bible. Dr. Walberg encouraged me through a personal letter to develop the habit of reading. Using himself as an example, he shared how he read the Bible for an hour each day. He also read a newspaper each day, a magazine each week, and a book each week. Hearing that, I decided to increase my

Bible reading beyond the minimum requirement for Campus Life to an hour each evening before bed. After all, I found that it was no longer a chore to do, but I really enjoyed it!

Since I enjoyed it so much, I decided to take my Bible to school. In my particular high school, this was really unheard of. Still, I had two hours of study hall each day that I wanted to use to read my Bible. Even with that, I kept my hour before bed so that I was reading the Bible for three hours each day.

As I continued to correspond with Pastor Walberg, he noted his habit of reading his Bible first thing in the morning to start his day off right. My habit had been to read in the evening and at school, so…I added another hour of Bible study in the morning to read four hours each day.

Finally, when I didn't have any sport that I was involved in, I added another hour each day right after school. If anything changed my life and washed me clean from the filthy lifestyle I had developed, it was the five hours each day of Bible study through much of my junior and senior years of high school. In fact, whereas I had been planning to study nuclear physics and join the Navy after high school, my plans changed. Now, I wanted to study the Bible more and more, so I dropped the plans for nuclear physics and ended up getting degrees in Bible and Biblical Studies. My life's trajectory had been set.

While still in high school, my life centered on evangelism. When I carried my Bible to school, I was no longer reading for myself alone. Others noticed, and they asked why a high school student would carry his Bible to school. My reading led to their hearing.

I also took the opportunity to witness to my skateboarding friends by writing Scripture verses on the top of my shoes to generate questions to increase the opportunities for witness.

But put on the Lord Jesus Christ, and make no provision for the flesh in regard to its lusts.

Romans 13:14 (NASB)

I have made a covenant with my eyes; How then could I gaze at a virgin?

Job 31:1 (NASB)

My skateboard had a dragon painted on it, so I scratched it out and plastered very clear Christian messages to steer my thinking away from the sinful lifestyle of many of my skateboarding friends and toward a lifestyle that honors and proclaims Christ as King.

I physically burned Satanic and secular music that I had previously listened to, such as Slayer, Metallica, AC/DC, and more. I was separating myself from the world systems that influenced my thinking toward hatred and evil.

In doing these things, I had to defend my faith from atheists who wanted nothing to do with God, secularists who were too busy for God, and even Satanists who, by their own admission, worshiped the devil himself. While I was wearing a provocative Christian T-shirt, someone threatened me in the hallway of my school, "By the end of the day, I'm going to burn that shirt off of you." Another day, while wearing a different Christian T-shirt, some boys crossed the street and ran toward my friend and me, shouting slurs against Christ and throwing stones at us. I was ostracized from many people in my school who had been my friends in my old party scene but did not appreciate this renewal in my life. I saw this persecution as the price to be paid for following Jesus.

After this, I went to a Christian college, the University of Northwestern in St. Paul, Minnesota. I learned a tremendous amount about the Bible in my four years there, and my faith continued to be refined and structured. My study of Scripture was switched into overdrive which changed my thought patterns and gave me even more conviction for the Lord. However, what I had in abundance of zeal, I lacked in relating to everyday people. As an example, I joined the evangelism team and spent Friday nights in downtown Minneapolis sharing my faith boldly in a confrontational manner in front of bars downtown. I was speaking with homosexuals and drug addicts and thieves and gang members, and I wasn't known for laying things out gently. While offering a Bible to one young woman, I was sharing how Jesus loved her and could walk with her out of a life of sin. Just then, her friend grabbed the Bible out of my hands, spit in it, and threw it into a gutter. Interestingly, this young woman rebuked her friend, saying how rude that was, and asked me if she could have *that specific Bible,* spit and all. I gave it to her but never saw her again. My prayer is that she actually read the book and was transformed like I was but having an even more gentle spirit like she showed that night.

During my second year at Northwestern, I had a major shift take place in my thinking during a world religions class with Dr. Sam Pittman. As I read about the millions and even billions of people in these other religions, I recognized that their story is substantially different from even the lost people I was evangelizing on the streets of Minneapolis. You see, in Minneapolis, there were many churches where people could go to learn about Jesus. If they were interested in Jesus, there were many Christian bookstores. If they were interested, there were many radio stations, many tracts being handed out on the streets, and even students like me sharing the truth with them directly. These people had the same spiritual condition as those in other religions:

they were lost. On the other hand, their access to the Gospel was far different. Virtually all of the people I evangelized in high school and college had heard about Jesus, had studied Christianity, or had even grown up in the Church, but they rejected it. I learned in my world religions class about billions of T.H.U.M.B. people, that is, Tribal (T), Hindu (H), Unreligious (U), Muslim (M), and Buddhist (B). They simply had never heard the Gospel. They had no opportunity to accept or reject Jesus because no one had ever told them about Jesus' offer of salvation in a way they could understand. I didn't learn that the technical term for these people is "Unreached" at the time, but it moved me that billions were going to hell without ever hearing about Jesus.

I share all of this from my own walk of faith because it is part of the story that shaped my thinking toward missions and evangelism as I have grown in Christ. To be candid, I didn't have an integral life. I was one-sided. I would have been one of those people who insisted on the duality discussed in this book, declaring that really spiritual, committed people should set aside "ordinary work" and dedicate themselves wholly to missions and evangelism. This would be expressed supremely by sacrificing one's career, skills, gifts, family, and education to live and then die on the mission field.

Although my zeal had some admirable qualities, my approach was simply incomplete. If someone would have asked me, "What is the mission of God's people?" I would have answered, "Of course, it's missions! The answer is in the question!" I would have naively voiced that every Christian should be sent to the Unreached as a missionary. I would have proclaimed along with Keith Green's song lyrics, "Jesus commands us to go. It should be the exception if we stay." Never mind the logistical impossibility of *everyone* going. Never mind the simple fact that followers of Jesus participate in and make key contributions to ordinary life right where they are without being sent anywhere. I passionately spoke to my friends to challenge them all to go.

In high school, I wanted those near me to have the same hope and joy and love that I had found in Christ. In college, I wanted all people everywhere to at least have the opportunity to hear about Jesus' sacrifice and decide for themselves whether they would like to follow him. I came from and lived in the traditional evangelism and missions world for many years. Over and over, I fell into the incomplete effort to bring people to Jesus in ten-minutes time to the neglect of the whole person. To be sure, there must be some point when people are challenged to take the step to believe, but focusing only on that point in evangelism is incomplete.

My hope now is that my story will help you to see the full, whole-life Good News that Jesus offers the world. My path is significant because it is the road the Lord used to lead me to the integral life with complete passion and purpose for God.

CHAPTER 13–WHY MISSIONS EXISTS

#BringThemIn

"Why should anyone hear the Gospel twice before everyone has heard it once?"

—Oswald J. Smith

I have laid out in this book that our whole lives serve Christ as we reflect the image of God as creators, curators, and cultivators. To be sure, we can reflect the character and nature of God through our art, order, and care readily wherever we are. However, when we consider that the vast majority of people in need of this message do not live in our immediate context, we must recognize that we need to go to where they are. These Majority World rest behind walls of geography, language, and politics that prevent them from hearing the Good News. That being the case, many of us need to take our art, order, and care there. It is not enough for us to be persuaded of these truths where we are, simply living them out as our service to God. Some of us are compelled to give all we can so that others at least have the option of knowing God as we do. Rather than leave them imprisoned behind barriers of deserts, islands, and mountains, some of us must cross those cultural barriers to share this Good News with them. This is my heartfelt plea that many reading this book will respond to this urgent call to take this message to them where they are.

The Ultimate Goal of Cross-Cultural Missions

In the autumn of 1990, I visited numerous churches in my first days at the University of Northwestern in St. Paul, Minnesota. Although I had attended a Converge Church (that is, Baptist General Conference) in my hometown, I wasn't looking just within my denomination. I sampled several "megachurches" that were charismatic, but I could not identify with their doctrinal belief that every believer would speak in tongues, for instance, so I kept searching for a church.

My first Sunday at Bethlehem Baptist Church was a crowded, cramped Sunday where there was standing room only in the balcony of the sanctuary because the church was in the midst of a major expansion into an entirely newly constructed section of the building. Parking was unavailable, requiring walking blocks through downtown Minneapolis. Building construction blocked normal entrances and exits, and my visit had all the external markings of pushing me on to try a different church. Even so, something in the early days of John Piper's preaching alighted in my heart, and that was, indeed, the last church I visited in my college years. Going forward, I never wavered from Bethlehem Baptist Church for the next four years, and my connection to Bethlehem had continued through regular sermon listening, partnership in ministry efforts over theological issues, and even mentoring when I was starting out as a pastor on my own in a small, country church.

It would be difficult to overestimate the impact of my tutelage under John Piper. One might even say that I learned as much theology from him as I did through my formal education. I hear his preaching style in my own. I repeat quotations and phrases I know I heard from him. I've wept with him and his wife Noel over a wayward family member, an apostate missionary, the death of an infant child, and the lost people of Minneapolis. I've even shared the shock of one of the associate pastors being pick-pocketed in the church parking lot while he was looking at the aforementioned construction work! Even so, I would esteem his greatest contribution to my life as the passion for the supremacy of God in cross-cultural missions.

This cross-cultural aspect of missionary work is in virtually every book that John Piper writes, to be sure, but his primary work on missions is *Let the Nations Be Glad: The Supremacy of God in Missions*. By way of an unorthodox beginning to the book, Dr. Piper begins,

> *Missions is not the ultimate goal of the church. Worship is. Missions exists because worship doesn't. Worship is ultimate, not missions, because God is ultimate, not man. When this age is over, and the countless millions of the redeemed fall on their faces before the throne of God, missions will be no more. It is a temporary necessity. But worship abides forever.*

It would seem that a book on missions would start with missions, rather than beginning by saying missions is not supreme. Yet, Piper is precisely correct. Indeed, a number of modern missions authors would do well to take heed to Piper's words even as they aim to generate more interest in missions.

Having served on the senior leadership team of a large mission agency, I've seen personally how many people are simply burned out and disillusioned either with missions itself or with the mission agency because of a misunderstood expectation that missions is their ultimate calling. Simply put, they misplace missions as the ultimate goal of the Church. They take up this call, go through the rigors of raising support, quitting jobs, sacrificing careers, moving families, learning language, enduring culture acquisition, but then finding that their "calling" isn't enough. They ask themselves, "Did I sacrifice all of this so that I could go to India and have a team leader say there's no place for my ministry in this country? Did I sacrifice all of this to have the Chinese government expel all teams from the country? Did I sacrifice all of this only to have my ministry team undermine my ministry by gossip? Did I sacrifice all of this to have my family scrape through five life-threatening illnesses in these few months?"

Others have looked at the task at hand and simply grown cold in their efforts or beliefs that God can reach "that people group." Some of these people have given up on missions entirely by assuming, for instance, that Muslims simply cannot be reached with the Gospel or that Russians are superior to American life and culture in every way, or the polygamy of Thai culture is too much to resist.

Without a doubt, these horror stories are not the typical experience or the norm in missions, but each of them is an accounting of a real incident that I have been personally connected with.

That being the case, what should mission agencies and mission pastors and mission committees do to prevent their missionaries from being these sorts of victims? One thing to do is to set the entire missionary endeavor into its rightful place: "Missions is not the ultimate goal of the church. Worship is. Missions exists because worship doesn't. Worship is ultimate, not missions, because God is ultimate, not man."

Of First Importance – Coda

Before anyone picks up on those last paragraphs and claims that I am against missions, I want to be careful to emphasize again that I am not discounting or diminishing the critical work of cross-cultural missions. Indeed, I have founded a missionary training organization myself, and I passionately urge people to give their lives to share the truth of the Gospel to the ends of the earth. That being said, I will also note that the overemphasis of the importance of cross-cultural missions has caused many to become disillusioned with the whole effort, throwing the baby out with the proverbial bathwater. At risk of repeating the argument from chapter three, let me share again the Apostle Paul's words,

> *For I passed on to you as of first importance what I also received—that Christ died for our sins according to the scriptures, and that he was buried, and that he was raised on the third day according to the scriptures, and that he appeared to Cephas, then to the twelve.*
>
> *1 Corinthians 15:3–*

From this, it is clear that whatever God's mission is for his people, the preaching of this Good News is the foremost aim of the Church. Moreover, cross-cultural missions is the culmination of many of the missions of God's people affirmed throughout *the integral life*.

Again, as noted in chapter three, even the significance of calling people to decision about the Gospel cannot be left to chance or implicit activity. The Gospel must be explicitly shared with all people everywhere. This is the very logic of Paul in Romans 10,

> *How are they to call on one they have not believed in? And how are they to believe in one they have not heard of? And how are they to hear without someone preaching to them?*
>
> *Romans 10:14*

So, it is imperative to affirm that the mission of God's people is no less than cross-cultural missions. But even this is a small slice of all that God has intended for his people and the human race as a whole.

A Flood of Knowledge

We've looked carefully at the cultural mandate and the commissions that God gave humanity in Genesis 1, namely, be fruitful, multiply, fill the earth, subdue it, and rule over it. Additionally, from Genesis 2, we were further commanded to care for and maintain it. However, through human disobedience, this did not happen. Even as representatives of God on earth bearing his image, we did not fulfill what we were commanded to do. In fact, in Genesis 11, it is recorded in the story of the Tower of Babel that humans directly rebelled against this command and did all they could to avoid being scattered over the face of the earth. This even included building a tower to assail heaven itself and unseat God from his throne.

From all of this, we can see that the glory of God is a critically important theme in the relations between God and humankind. It is so important to God that Scripture assures that his glory will be manifest throughout the earth even in spite of the disobedience of humankind. The Scriptural evidence is almost overwhelming:

- *But truly, as I live, all the earth will be filled with the glory of the Lord.*—Numbers 14:21
- *Let all the people of the earth acknowledge the LORD and turn to him! Let all the nations worship you!*—Psalm 22:27
- *His glorious name deserves praise forevermore. May his majestic splendor fill the whole earth. We agree! We agree!*—Psalm 72:19
- *He, the very one who descended, is also the one who ascended above all the heavens, in order to fill all things.*—Ephesians 4:10
- *Now the church is his body, the fullness of him who fills all in all.*—Ephesians 1:23
- *They called out to one another, "Holy, holy, holy is the Lord of Heaven's Armies! His majestic splendor fills the entire earth!"*—Isaiah 6:3
- *He promotes equity and justice; the Lord's faithfulness extends throughout the earth.*—Psalm 33:5
- *The LORD will then be king over all the earth. In that day the LORD will be seen as one with a single name.*—Zechariah 14:9
- *They will no longer injure or destroy on my entire royal mountain. For there will be universal submission to the Lord's sovereignty, just as the waters completely cover the sea.*—Isaiah 11:9
- *For recognition of the Lord's sovereign majesty will fill the earth just as the waters fill up the sea.*—Habakkuk 2:14
- *God comes from Teman, the Holy One from Mount Paran. Selah. His splendor has covered the skies, the earth is full of*

his glory.—Habakkuk 3:3

All of that being said, Scripture continues its overwhelming evidence of the glory of the Lord being made manifest through the very nations that God created:

- *All the nations, whom you created, will come and worship you, O Lord. They will honor your name.*—Psalm 86:9
- *Then those living on earth will know what you are like; all nations will know how you deliver your people.*—Psalm 67:2
- *The LORD demonstrates his power to deliver; in the sight of the nations he reveals his justice. He remains loyal and faithful to the family of Israel. All the ends of the earth see our God deliver us.*—Psalm 98:2–3
- *Who will not fear you, O Lord, and glorify your name, because you alone are holy? All nations will come and worship before you for your righteous acts have been revealed.*—Revelation 15:4
- *As a result God highly exalted him and gave him the name that is above every name, so that at the name of Jesus every knee will bow —in heaven and on earth and under the earth— and every tongue confess that Jesus Christ is Lord to the glory of God the Father.*—Philippians 2:9–11
- *They were singing a new song: "You are worthy to take the scroll and to open its seals because you were killed, and at the cost of your own blood you have purchased for God persons from every tribe, language, people, and nation."*—Revelation 5:9
- *After these things I looked, and here was an enormous crowd that no one could count, made up of persons from every na-*

> *tion, tribe, people, and language, standing before the throne and before the Lamb dressed in long white robes, and with palm branches in their hands.*—Revelation 7:9

The bottom line is this: in order to have "*an enormous crowd that no one could count, made up of persons from every nation, tribe, people, and language*" (Revelation 7:9), each of you needs to "*confess with your mouth that Jesus is Lord and believe in your heart that God raised him from the dead*" (Romans 10:9). This is without debate.

Nevertheless, these passages of Scripture do not describe the state of affairs in the world today. We cannot look at the world today with 3.23 billion people in 4,595 people groups[62] that have no reasonable access to the Gospel and say that this lines up with the created vision we read in the above Scripture passages. We cannot say the job is complete when forty-four percent of the people groups of the world have not heard the Gospel in a way they can understand.

Made in His Image

All of those billions of people are, likewise, made in the image of God and given the created calling to reflect his image just as we do. Yet, without someone to go to them, they will never recognize their roles as creators, curators, and cultivators. They will never acknowledge Christ as Savior and bow to him in glad service and delight.

As it is now, some people are feasting on the Good News through churches, radio stations, Bible societies, seminaries, Christian bookstores, Christian conferences, and the list goes on. All the

---

62 Joshua Project, "People Group and Great Commission Statistics: Joshua Project," People Group and Great Commission statistics | Joshua Project, accessed December 10, 2020, https://joshuaproject.net/people_groups/statistics.

while, roughly half of the world has no reasonable access to hear the Good News even once. Oswald J. Smith, the founder of the People's Church of Toronto, Canada, preached, "We talk about the second blessing. They haven't had the first blessing yet. We talk about the second coming of Christ. They haven't heard about the first coming yet. It just isn't fair. 'Why should anyone hear the Gospel twice before everyone has heard it once?'"[63]

Of course, I would be the last person to say that we should not be feasting on the Gospel. We should be feasting and living and breathing the Gospel all day, every day. The point is that we have failed to prioritize everyone hearing the Gospel. Can we say with full integrity that this Good News has been given first importance in our lives? If it had been given first importance, it would be evident when this Good News permeates everything we do, and we would be shouting its truth from the rooftops.

Charles Peace was a notorious murderer of the 19th century. He was sentenced to death, but nonetheless, spoke powerful words on the morning of his execution,

> *Before him went the prison chaplain, routinely and sleepily reading some Bible verses. The criminal touched the preacher and asked what he was reading. "The Consolations of Religion," was the reply. Charlie Peace was shocked at the way he professionally read about hell. Could a man be so unmoved under the very shadow of the scaffold as to lead a fellow-human there and yet, dry-eyed, read of a pit that has no bottom into*

63 Oswald J Smith, "Why Should Anyone Hear the Gospel Twice before Everyone Has Heard It Once?," The Passion for Souls, accessed April 23, 2022, https://eending-joernaal.webflow.io/blog/why-should-anyone-hear-the-gospel-twice-before-everyone-has-heard-it-once.

which this fellow must fall? Could this preacher believe the words that there is an eternal fire that never consumes its victims, and yet slide over the phrase without a tremor? Is a man human at all who can say with no tears, "You will be eternally dying and yet never know the relief that death brings"? All this was too much for Charlie Peace. So he preached. Listen to his on-the-eve-of-hell sermon.

"Sir," addressing the preacher, "if I believed what you and the church of God say that you believe, even if England were covered with broken glass from coast to coast, I would walk over it, if need be, on hands and knees and think it worthwhile living, just to save one soul from an eternal hell like that!"[64]

Charlie Peace understood more of the impact of the Gospel than many professing Christians. If God paid the ultimate price for our salvation, we had better be willing to sacrifice everything to experience that salvation. If we experience the ultimate joy of salvation, we had better be willing to do all we can for others to enjoy that salvation. As Nancy Pearcey writes, "We should strive to develop a character of such a quality that people can see a difference between the redeemed and the unredeemed."[65] Can people see the difference in you through your passion for those who have never heard?

64 Leonard Ravenhill, *Why Revival Tarries* (Bloomington, MN: Bethany House Publishers, 2004), 33.

65 Nancy Pearcey, *Total Truth: Liberating Christianity from Its Cultural Captivity* (Wheaton, IL: Crossway Books, 2008), 91.

CHAPTER 14–YOUR CROSS OF GOLD

#BeTheThreshold

I grew up listening to Michael W. Smith as one of my favorite artists. For a young teenager, his lyrics were challenging to me personally and gave me something of an anthem to mark my life by those powerful words.

One of the songs I acutely remember was *Cross of Gold*. I think one of the reasons this song stood out to me was that it challenged me in something that I personally favored. I wore a cross of gold, and I was all about outward symbols to demonstrate the sincerity of my faith. Then, along comes one of my favorite performers who challenged that thinking and pointed out that merely wearing a cross of gold around your neck was not necessarily a good thing.

As the song points out, there's nothing inherently wrong with wearing a cross as a piece of jewelry. Nonetheless, there's nothing inherently good about wearing a cross as a piece of jewelry. No one gets brownie points before God for being visible about their faith. That being said, *the same act can honor the Lord or dishonor the Lord or neither.*

In fact, this teaching was part of the Sermon on the Mount,

> *Be careful not to display your righteousness merely to be seen by people. Otherwise you have no reward with your Father in heaven. Thus whenever you do charitable giving, do not blow a trumpet before you, as the hypocrites do in synagogues and on streets so that people will praise them. I tell you the truth, they have their reward! But when you do your giving, do not let your left hand know what your right hand is doing, so that your gift may be in secret. And your Father, who sees in secret, will reward you.*
>
> *Matthew 6:1–4*

So, Jesus does not teach that we should stop giving to the needy. Rather, like a skilled surgeon, he slices right to our heart's intentions by teaching us not to do these things *in order to be seen by others*. There are people who have those intentions. We should not be like them. Rather, we should give, to be sure! But we should do it with proper motives and intentions to help people, not to be rewarded with accolades for our so-called generous giving.

In a similar manner, there are people who wear religious emblems because it is fashionable or simply the thing to do. They want to be noticed, so they wear them because friends do or because it looks good at church or in youth group. This does not honor God. In the words of Jesus, "*they have received their reward.*"

Let me illustrate this in yet another way,

> *The rest of humanity, who had not been killed by these plagues, did not repent of the works of*

their hands, so that they did not stop worshiping demons and idols made of gold, silver, bronze, stone, and wood—idols that cannot see or hear or walk about. Furthermore, they did not repent of their murders, of their magic spells, of their sexual immorality, or of their stealing.

Revelation 9:20–21

Work is good when it is done with the right intention to honor God and fulfill the cultural mandate he gave to all humanity. On the other hand, this passage shows that the "*works of [our] hands*" can represent worshiping demons and idols. There is a binary switch determined by our intentions whether our work serves God on the one hand or serves demons on the other hand. An architect can design a building that is magnificent in its structure and beauty. If that masterpiece is constructed *with the intention of honoring himself*, it is worshiping demons because it is idolatry. If the same building is constructed *with the intention of honoring God* through the use of the architect's gifts, it is worshiping the Creator. For glory, intention determines direction.

That being the case, there are those who wear religious emblems or jewelry or make statements of faith very intentionally because of the meaning to them personally. Even more, people might do these same things because they open doors to a conversation about spiritual matters. Others simply wear them as reminders knowing that they will be visible to people who would notice, and the wearer wants to be numbered among those who follow Jesus. Let me share the story of two people who wore emblems of faith with intention.

Heroes of the Faith

From my college days in Minnesota in the early 1990s, there were plenty of students who adorned the walls of their dorm rooms with posters that celebrated heroes of the Christian faith. Posters of Michael W. Smith certainly graced some of those walls, as did Twila Paris, First Call, Stryper, Petra, DC Talk, Michael English, and so on.

My perspective of heroes of the Christian faith was defined a bit differently than other students, however. We had the very special privilege of having Richard and Sabina Wurmbrand speak to our student body during a chapel talk. If you don't know the Wurmbrands, they were like the reality TV stars of communist Romania. They were heroes across the country and even the whole communist world. Together, Richard and Sabina started the organization Voice of the Martyrs to advocate for those being persecuted for their faith in Christ.

In this chapel talk, Richard shared how he was arrested under communist rule in Romania and served fourteen years in prison for the "crime" of declaring that communism and Christianity were incompatible. During those years, Sabina repeatedly had government officials attempt to deceive her by coming to her door to give her the news that her husband was dead as another casualty of torture and deprivation in prison, but she refused to believe it. They urged her to recant her faith and simply move on to marry someone else, but she was unrelenting.

In reality, Richard was being repeatedly tortured in prison, as he documented in his book *Tortured for Christ*. The details of his torture are sickening, and when he was ransomed from prison, he and Sabina were allowed to emigrate to America. In the United States, Richard bore witness to the atrocities being committed against Christians in communist Romania. In fact, he testified before the US Senate and even stripped to the waist to show the deep scars that the instruments of torture inflicted on his body during his years in prison. In a very real sense, Richard could say with the Apostle Paul, "*I bear the marks of Jesus on my body*" (Galatians 6:17).

Richard and Sabina Wurmbrand were heroes of the Christian faith for me. Sitting across the table with them for lunch and sensing their love and care for an eighteen-year-old college student left an indelible impact on my life.

That being the case, I wanted to celebrate these heroes. I wanted to be regularly reminded of their "Cross of Gold" and their personal advice and care for me. After their departure, I surreptitiously took down one of the posters with their picture on it that had advertised their speaking engagements and hung it on the wall of my dorm room. These were people I could celebrate far more than the 1990s Christian rock bands with their massive sprayed hairdos impervious to gale-force winds.

Most of us don't bear in our bodies the marks of Jesus. Short of bearing those marks, we do have means of reminding ourselves of our walk with God. Likewise, we have means of showing others that we are followers of God. In fact, the Bible encourages that sort of theological two-step from the outset of God's call and command to Abraham.

Inside-Outside Faith

One of the most famous passages of Scripture for the Jewish people is Deuteronomy 6,

> *Hear, O Israel: The Lord is our God, the Lord is one! You must love the Lord your God with your whole mind, your whole being, and all*

> *your strength.*
>
> *These words I am commanding you today must be kept in mind, and you must teach them to your children and speak of them as you sit in your house, as you walk along the road, as you lie down, and as you get up. You should tie them as a reminder on your forearm and fasten them as symbols on your forehead. Inscribe them on the doorframes of your houses and gates.*
>
> *Deuteronomy 6:4*

This passage of Scripture is so well-known, in fact, that it has a special name being called the *Shema. Shema* is the Hebrew word for "hear" that starts out the passage, but it has an important sense that should not be overlooked. *Shema* would not be used simply to describe a noise that was heard in the woods or even the hearing of music. It is not merely physiological. Rather, *shema* means to "hear and obey."

For example, when a parent tells a child to take out the trash and the parent verifies that the child isn't going to come up with excuses, the parent might ask, "Did you hear what I said?" The parent is not asking whether the child physiologically heard the percussive sound waves reverberate through the air over the noise of the child's video game. The parent is ensuring that the child will *listen and obey.*

Deuteronomy 6 is not commanding people to be especially attentive to background noises. This passage is commanding people to *listen and obey.* What follows, then, is a powerful statement of the unity of God and the bottom-line command of God to love the Lord with everything a person has. Next, the directive to listen and obey incorporates the specific commands that Moses has taught the people so that they will not drift away from the Lord. To effect that permeation of all of life, Moses adjures the Jewish people to repeat the commands, discuss the commands diligently at all times and in all imaginable activities.

The next phrases seem a bit out of place to modern readers, so they are worth repeating here for explanation:

> *You should tie them as a reminder on your forearm and fasten them as symbols on your forehead. Inscribe them on the doorframes of your houses and gates.*

What's this business about tying the commands on forearms and foreheads? What's the difference between doorframes and gates?

In answer to this, let me ask a question to demonstrate. Imagine a day many years ago when people did not have cell phones. If you met someone new who gave you their phone number, but you didn't have paper to write it, where would you write it? Often, that phone number would be inked on the back of your hand. On the other hand, would a stranger read a number off of your wrist? Not likely. So, it is clear, the back of the hand is for the individual.

Now, imagine another time long ago before virtually everyone carried smartphones with reversible cameras. If you smudged your fingers with ink and then you touched your forehead spreading the smudge from your fingers, whom would you ask about whether your forehead had a colorful imprint? You would ask your neighbor, or at least the person next to you, because most of us are not able to bend our eyes to see our foreheads. The forehead, then, is something others see.

What the Jews have is the command to keep visual reminders of the commands of Moses on the back of their hands *for their own benefit* so that they remember all that he commanded. In addition, they have the command to keep visual reminders of the commands of Moses on their foreheads as notable *symbols of their identity for the benefit of others* so that they know who the followers of God are.

As though these two examples were not enough for this principle, Moses gives another image that is perfectly clear in the Middle Eastern mind. Having lived in the Middle East for a number of years, I am very familiar with the walled exterior of properties. In fact, in some municipalities, a wall is a legal requirement for every property, whether it might be a twelve-foot wall such as those that surrounded Osama bin Laden's hideout or a two-foot decorative wall that could easily be stepped over. Nonetheless, virtually every property has an external gate through the walls to enter the *hosh*, or "garden." It is inside the garden that family activities take place. This is where children play in safety and where food is served and where the family's animals are kept. To enter the home, of course, a person passes through another door from the *hosh* to the home, passing the doorpost of the house itself.

So again, Moses gives a word picture to write the commands on the gates of *the walls that everyone else sees so that they can identify the people* as followers of God. Not only that, but they were to write the commands *on the doorposts of the house that only the family and guests see so that all are reminded* of their identity as followers of God.

Both of these examples, then, from one of the most important texts in all of the Hebrew Bible, encourage the people of God to identify themselves as the people of God to outsiders and to remind themselves that they are the people of God as insiders.

To be sure, there are elements of this passage that are culturally bound to the specific Hebrew people. Indeed, the very next verse refers to the physical land of Israel as an inheritance and the physical fathers of these people of Abraham, Isaac, and Jacob. That being said, the principle of identifying yourself as a follower of God to outsiders and reminding yourself that you are a follower of God certainly seems to be a transcultural principle that crosses the boundaries of time, geography, and even ethnic groups. At least in this way, we can learn a powerful lesson from the Jewish *Shema*.

Wear Your Witness

Knowing the background of the *Shema*, I am even more of a fan of intentional symbols of faith. Mark those words carefully, though. They are *intentional* symbols of faith. For example, on my wrist, I wear a simple bracelet that has about a dozen names of Jesus written on it. Throughout the day, I might be standing in line at the post office or sitting at a red light in traffic, and I will read and meditate on those names. This is an intentional reminder to me of who I am as a follower of the Lord, and it nurtures my walk with him day by day.

I also carry with me an Amazon Kindle virtually everywhere I go. From the screen itself, I have access to hundreds of thousands of pages of books. On the reverse side, I have taped a picture of 1 Timothy 2:5 in Arabic,

اللهُ وَاحِدٌ، وَلَا شَفِيعَ بَيْنَهُ وَبَيْنَ النَّاسِ إِلَّا الْإِنْسَانُ الْمَسِيحُ عِيسَى

> *For there is one God and one intermediary between God and humanity, Christ Jesus, himself human...*

Because much of my ministry has focused on Arabs, this is an identifier to them that I am a follower of Jesus. People notice their own language when they are visiting a foreign country. Their eyes gravitate to it and fix on it even across a room. Regarding this verse, for example, one old man saw that I had displayed it and stopped to talk to me for some time. I spoke to him in Arabic even though we were in Orlando, Florida. He called over his wife and his two sons and their wives and his grandchildren. He then had me explain to all of them what I had told him: there is only one God, and there is one mediator between us and God who made so great a sacrifice that He could remove all the wrong things we did. As we parted, he left with a smile saying, "I like this. I will remember this. Kids, you remember this."

All of this came from my own simple *Shema* statement. I want to challenge you with something similar. What will be your *Shema*? How will you regularly identify yourself to others as a follower of Jesus? How will you regularly remind yourself of your need to obey all he commanded?

Let me give a few examples of how you could use these *with intention*:

1. Asking, "Could I pray for you right now?" shows that prayer is important beyond just a surface prayer at meals.

2. When someone asks you, "How are you?" Respond, "Better than I deserve." This opens the door to discuss grace vs. deserved condemnation.

3. In response to the question, "Why don't you have a spouse/kids/a son?" respond, "God hasn't sent me one yet, and I trust that he knows what's best for me."

4. Focus on the meanings of names. For example, I know

that "Abdullah" means "servant of God." In a New York City taxi, I mentioned to my taxi driver, "Oh, your name is Abdullah. That means 'servant of God.' So, how do you serve God?" At first, he didn't understand, but I explained how I serve God by reading the Bible and praying and caring for my family and working hard at my job and telling other people about God. His pensive response was, "This is a good question."

5. Finding proverbs with deep meaning can serve as *Shema* statements. One friend uses the Turkish proverb, "I've never seen a man without any clothes, but I've seen many clothes that contain no man." This can then lead to a discussion about deeper things.

6. We've hosted about a dozen foreign exchange students in our home from Saudi Arabia and the United Arab Emirates. We've said to them, "I love the Emirates, but I love Emiratis (the people of the Emirates) more." This leads to a discussion of why we would love them.

7. Rephrasing religious phrases to inject new meaning or catch attention, whereas the rote phrases might just pass over. For example, when my friend sneezes and someone says, "God bless you," he replies, "He does! Thank you!"

8. Expressing gratitude beyond a simple "thank you" directs appreciation to the Lord, "Ah, thank you, Lord! Isn't a simple cup of coffee a blessing?"

9. Making a connection with someone while thanking them for a service directs them to God, "Thank you, my friend. I am blessed by God through your friendship."

10. When complaints and problems are mentioned, simply asking why they think bad things happen moves the dis-

cussion to Genesis and how sin came into the world.

11. If you are speaking with Jews or Muslims who greet you with "Shalom" or "Salaam," you can greet them back, but then ask, "Where does real peace come from?" Many pat answers simply don't address true peace with God.

12. "You are not smiling today. What is happening with you?" This can be coupled with, "I'll pray for that."

13. With five children, one of my favorite *Shema* statements has been the Scripture, "*Children are a gift from the Lord*" (Psalm 127:3). I spoke this to a woman bagging our groceries, and she simply stopped and said, "You know, that is absolutely true. I need to remember that!" She then accepted my offer to study the Bible with our family.

14. Similar to the *Shema* statements of gratefulness above, simply recognize that God is providing everything we need.

15. Earnestly saying, "May God bless you and your family," can turn someone's perspective toward God.

16. Even phrases like, "May the peace (grace, blessing, joy, love) of the Lord Jesus be with you and your family" were commonplace not so long ago. How would these be perceived in your context?

17. When meeting foreigners, ask, "Do you know that God has a specific plan to bless your country and people?" Revelation 5:9 and Revelation 7:9 show the end result of every people and nation and tribe and tongue being blessed by his Son.

18. Rephrasing Jesus' words that he first chose us, "I love God because he loved me first."

19. Simply asking, "Can I tell you an interesting Bible story

I read recently?"

20. Saying, "I am a follower of Jesus, so I often pray for people I meet. Do you have something I can pray for you about?"

21. Especially when talking with people whose culture doesn't value women, a man could say, "This is a photo of my wife. She is the second greatest gift God has given me!" This affirms godly marriage as well as opens the door to conversation about salvation being the greatest gift.

22. When someone wrongs you or makes a mistake, then reply, "If that's the worst thing that happens to me today, then it is a great day!" It's not overtly spiritual, but people are pleasantly shocked by the positive attitude. Then, the response can be more centered on God.

23. When meeting immigrants, say, "God gave me a love for Somali people," for example.

24. If someone asks, "What country are you from?" You can respond, "Heaven. Well, at least that's where I'm a citizen." This is based on Philippians 3:20, "*But our citizenship is in heaven, and from it we await a Savior, the Lord Jesus Christ…*"

25. A good friend of mine likes to share, "What a beautiful day! And God gives it to us for free!"

Of course, there are myriad other ideas like bumper stickers, doormats, decorative verses on walls, a cross at your home, and yes, even wearing a cross of gold. These can all serve the purpose of reminding us of who we are as followers of Jesus while also identifying us as followers of Jesus.

The Core of Conversion

There is another reason to wear your witness, so to speak, but it takes some explanation. In short, wearing your witness makes you part of the social network of believers in a pre-believer's life, which makes their profession much more reasonable. This point requires some history, analysis, and application.

Many have looked at the first three centuries of Christianity and wondered at the dynamic, almost incredible growth of the religion from an extremely small, persecuted minority religion in Palestine to the predominant religion of the entire Roman Empire spanning from present-day Great Britain to Morocco to Iraq to Romania to Germany and everything in between. To be sure, it is a legitimate question. How did Christianity grow so dynamically? Was it through amazing acts of bravery like Richard and Sabina Wurmbrand displayed that caused a groundswell of belief to pervade whole people groups? Was the growth through repeated mass conversion events of thousands of people through sermons like the day of Pentecost in Acts 2? Was it through "natural growth" where Christians simply outpaced the rest of the population in producing children who, in turn, followed the faith of their parents? Or was it a steady, measured growth of conversion where more and more people were persuaded by the active, living faith of Christianity's proponents?

Dr. Rodney Stark is a professor of history at Baylor University who has written numerous books to answer these questions. Even as a sociologist and a historian, though, he has creatively stepped out of his own discipline to look at these questions through statistical analysis. From the historical side, he can look at census lists or graveyards to identify Christian names and trace those names to identify the gradual growth of Christianity. On the other hand, from the statistical side, he answers creative and seemingly inane questions about how Christianity grew successfully in urban Roman cities or urban Roman cities on coasts or urban Roman cities on coasts with a history of Egyptian religion and so on.

Find Us Faithful

One of the elements I find so encouraging about Stark's findings is the number 3.42 percent. What's so significant about this number? By Stark's analysis, he shows that a growth rate of 3.42 percent per year can account for the reported 6.2 million followers of Christ in the Roman Empire by AD 300.[66]

Of course, from the history of Scripture recorded throughout the New Testament, we know that there were numerous miraculous bursts of growth far more than the minimum 3.42 percent. For me, however, this remains a good number because it shows the feasibility of faithful Christians sharing the truth of the Gospel in everyday life and seeing a dramatic, cumulative effect. Far from explaining away any miraculous growth of Christianity, 3.42 percent represents the faithful witness of common people who took Christianity from a minuscule group to becoming the predominant religion of the Roman empire. Indeed, it represents hope that faithfully following Jesus today can result in massive world-impacting growth.

As noted, Stark's analysis represents a minimum starting point and excludes miraculous bursts of growth, such as we see in Acts 2. This was by intention so that his analysis could withstand rigorous academic scrutiny, but as believers, we trust the integrity of Scripture, and we recognize that these "minimum" figures are enhanced exponentially by the miracles recounted in Scripture. Indeed, the Lord sovereignly moves on hearts, so 3.42 percent is

66 Rodney Stark, *The Rise of Christianity: How the Obscure, Marginal Jesus Movement Became the Dominant Religious Force in the Western World in a Few Centuries* (San Francisco, CA: Harper Collins Publishers, 1997), 6-7.

not a formula for growth. Rather, when those miracles are coupled with the steady growth figure of 3.42 percent, the growth of the Church is not only plausible but almost undeniable. In this way, we can be encouraged by punctuations of miraculous moves of the Lord along with the faithful witness of everyday followers of Jesus.

To that end, the following table illustrates these steady growth projections by starting with very conservative numbers, fewer than those accounted for in the book of Acts. Indeed, by AD 350, the population of followers of Jesus was 33.88 million people. That is, Christians comprised 56.5 percent of the total Roman Empire, which accords with numerous other descriptions of the total Roman Empire.

Table 1.1		
Christian Growth Projected at 40 Percent per Decade		
Year	Number of Christians	Percent of Population
40	1,000	0.0017
50	1,400	0.0023
100	7,530	0.0126
150	40,496	0.07
200	217,795	0.36
250	1,171,356	1.9
300	6,299,832	10.5
350	33,882,008	56.5
*Based on an estimated population of 60 million		Credit: Rodney Starks

Of course, it must be kept in mind that projections like this do not follow a perfectly linear growth pattern, so Stark's numbers show only that this was *one possible* way the population could have grown. By his own admission, there were bumps and jumps along the way, so it is not a smooth "hockey stick" growth curve. In fact, some of those bumps and jumps are the most interesting and salient points of Stark's study that pertain to *the integral life*. When devastating tragedies hit, it was then that the Church lived out the integral life of interdependence and faithful witness through all of life, and God used that to grow his Church through the ages.

Faithful Living in Plagues and Pandemics

> *"For the fact is that typically people do not seek a faith; they encounter one through their ties to other people who already accept this faith."*[67]

Rodney Stark presents a compelling analysis[68] on this matter with the following key conclusion: epidemics had the dramatic effect of propelling the adoption of Christianity throughout the Roman Empire.

First, there are two significant pandemics that occurred in the early centuries of Christianity that revealed elements of the Christian faith that set it apart from all other religions. The pandemics focused on are the appearance of what was likely smallpox in A.D. 165, known as the Antonine Plague, and the likely appearance of measles in A.D. 251 during the Plague of Cyprian. It is estimated that each of these two pandemics *killed up*

67 Rodney Stark, *The Rise of Christianity: How the Obscure, Marginal Jesus Movement Became the Dominant Religious Force in the Western World in a Few Centuries* (San Francisco, CA: Harper Collins Publishers, 1997), 56.
68 Ibid., Chapter 4, "Epidemics, Networks, and Conversion".

to one-third of the total population. Some accounts have it that death visited *every household,* and many households were completely obliterated with every person being killed.

Of course, it must be noted that none of the modern conventions of hospitals or sanitation or vaccines were available, but neither was there even a basic understanding of germ theory. No one knew how the diseases were passed from one person to another, so when loved ones began to show any symptoms whatsoever, they were thrown into the piles of dead corpses in the streets *while still alive.* For those among the pagans who had the means, they simply ran from the disease retreating to rural areas less impacted by the ensuing death. This not only included aristocracy but pagan priests as well. Having no explanation for the onslaught of the disease and having no cure for it, and recognizing they had no god who was greater than it, the pagan priests themselves simply abandoned the populace and isolated themselves as much as possible from those affected.

Contrast that response with the response of Christians. First, Christians believed that Jesus brought them eternal salvation so that even in death, they had hope. "Christianity offered a much more satisfactory account of why these terrible times had fallen upon humanity, and it projected a hopeful, even enthusiastic, portrait of the future."[69]

Second, Christian doctrine provided a prescription for action. "When disasters struck, the Christians were better able to cope, and this resulted in *substantially higher rates of survival.* This meant that in the aftermath of each pandemic, Christians made up a larger percentage of the population even without new con-

---

69 Rodney Stark, *The Rise of Christianity: How the Obscure, Marginal Jesus Movement Became the Dominant Religious Force in the Western World in a Few Centuries* (San Francisco, CA: Harper Collins Publishers, 1997), 74.

verts" (ibid.).

The third point is that Christian values of love and charity were more than mere lip service. The following is an extended quotation from Dyonisius written around 260:

> *Most of our brother Christians showed unbounded love and loyalty, never sparing themselves and thinking only of one another. Heedless of danger, they took charge of the sick, attending to their every need and ministering to them in Christ, and with them departed this life serenely happy; for they were infected by others with the disease, drawing on themselves the sickness of their neighbors and cheerfully accepting their pains. Many, in nursing and curing others, transferred their death to themselves and died in their stead... The best of our brothers lost their lives in this manner, a number of presbyters, deacons, and laymen winning high commendation so that death in this form, the result of great piety and strong faith, seems in every way the equal of martyrdom.*[70]

Notably, this care for people was not spent only on those fellow Christians. Certain passages of Scripture might lead us to believe that our acts of service and care are to be directed only to brothers and sisters in the faith. For example,

> *For I was hungry and you gave me food, I was thirsty and you gave me something to drink, I was a stranger and you invited me in, I was naked*

70 Ibid., 82.

and you gave me clothing, I was sick and you took care of me, I was in prison and you visited me.' Then the righteous will answer him, 'Lord, when did we see you hungry and feed you, or thirsty and give you something to drink? When did we see you a stranger and invite you in, or naked and clothe you? When did we see you sick or in prison and visit you?' And the king will answer them, 'I tell you the truth, just as you did it for one of the least of these brothers or sisters of mine, you did it for me.'

Matthew 25:35–40

The believers, through these plagues, did not seem to exclude their service and care for only their brothers and sisters in the faith. Indeed, they did care for their fellow Christians, but it seems that their care extended far beyond their fellow Christians to anyone who needed mercy and care, much like Galatians 6:10 commands,

So then, whenever we have an opportunity, let us do good to all people, and especially to those who belong to the family of faith.

Even the pagan emperor Julian noticed the good deeds of the Christian believers and complained when comparing them to the pagans, "The impious Galileans [Christians] support not only their poor, but ours as well, everyone can see that our people lack aid from us."[71]

71 Rodney Stark, *The Rise of Christianity: How the Obscure, Marginal Jesus Movement Became the Dominant Religious Force in the Western World in a Few Centuries* (San Francisco, CA: Harper Collins Publishers, 1997), 84.

So, the followers of Jesus were indiscriminate in their compassion and care for those who had need. They even carried out this indiscriminate care at risk to themselves. But how much could simple nursing care do without an understanding of germ theory or antibiotics or sanitation? Quite a bit can be done, in fact. Stark notes, "modern medical experts believe that conscientious nursing *without any medications* could cut the mortality rate by two-thirds or even more."[72] Keeping people warm and administering food and water allows the immune system just enough aid to begin to heal.

Yet, in doing so, they reduced the mortality rate among Christians from thirty percent to ten percent. Where they cared for pagans, their mortality rate was reduced from thirty percent to ten percent. For those pagans who did not have this care, the mortality rate remained a devastating thirty percent which meant that the per capita percentage of the populace that followed Christ grew enormously on account of these pandemics. Not only that, but the pagans who did survive witnessed the sacrificial service of the Christians. By the end of these pandemics in the latter half of the third century, virtually everyone in the urban Roman Empire was a Christian, had been nursed back to health by a Christian, or knew someone who had been nursed back to health by a Christian.

The end result of this is that Christians ran to the pandemics at risk of their own lives to live out the Gospel. In short, Christians were the "first responders," the heroes of these pandemics. They did this at certain risk to their own lives and those of their loved ones, knowing they might be taking on the very disease they hoped to help cure.

---

72 Ibid., 89.

The Threshold of Faith

One final note regarding the devastation of the plagues is that of attachments. Today, we associate attachments with cultural identity. For example, we refer to the Pashtun people of Afghanistan as High Identity Muslim People, or we refer to the Dravidian people of India as High Identity Hindu People. What is meant by this is that their social network of personal attachments is so strong that they are prevented from choosing another religion *even if they were persuaded*. The cultural attachments and expectations from fathers, mothers, grandparents, sisters, brothers, children, aunts, uncles, and friends prevent them from the freedom to choose a different religion because their identity is so tightly defined by these social attachments.

This was a similar scenario in the pagan Roman Empire. However, these pandemics loosened and/or eliminated the social attachments through the death of so many of the populace. Before the pandemic, a pagan's social network might have included five very close attachments, one with a Christian and four with pagans. Subtracting mortality and flight on account of the pandemic, the same person's social attachments would have changed dramatically. "What has happened is that where once there were four pagans to one Christian in this pagan's intimate circle, now there is, in effect, one of each—a dramatic equalization."[73] Even at that, it must be considered how many of the surviving pagans had been nursed back to health by Christians. This made the decision to convert to Christianity that much more reasonable since the resistance of those social attachments was dramatically weakened by the pandemic while at the same time dramatically strengthened with Christian associates.

---

73 Rodney Stark, *The Rise of Christianity: How the Obscure, Marginal Jesus Movement Became the Dominant Religious Force in the Western World in a Few Centuries* (San Francisco, CA: Harper Collins Publishers, 1997), 92.

Long before Facebook, Twitter, and Instagram, these attachments were the real social networks. Changing the cultural identity of surrounding people to 56.5 percent followers of Christ made it that much easier for remaining non-believers to follow Jesus. That threshold moved lower and lower so that acting on faith was less like scaling a wall and more like stepping over a speed bump. People were free to make a life-changing decision based on conscience.

One of the most encouraging aspects of this perspective on conversion is probably the most discomfiting aspect for "professional mission agencies." That fact is that "most conversions are not produced by professional missionaries, but by rank-and-file members who share their faith with their friends and relatives."[74] This is so fulfilling and encouraging because it speaks to the everyday, ordinary believer. Those are the people who are sharing who they are through *Shema* statements or through acts of mercy and care during times of people's deepest needs. It is through that care and love and living out the Gospel that people see the transforming power of the Gospel message. That is the real substance of this book, namely, that it is through whole-life Christianity that the mission of God's people will be carried out. This *integral life* approach includes art, order, and care. It includes work, family, and friendship. It does not necessitate being a "professional" minister to minister the Gospel to people in need.

Of course, this is not to denigrate the important work that professional ministers such as missionaries and pastors do. Missionaries with financial support have the freedom to go places where others might not be able to go to break new ground among Unreached People Groups. Indeed, focusing missionary efforts on this pioneering, apostolic work might be the clarion call to action for professional missionaries. Likewise, pastors with fi-

74 Rodney Stark, *Cities of God: Christianizing the Urban Empire* (San Francisco, CA: Harper Collins, 2006), 12.

nancial support have the freedom to apply more of their time to meeting the needs of the church and reaching those that may have been neglected. Even so, the point must be taken that all believers are called to be ministers of the Gospel through whole, integral lives.

Summary

Wearing your witness is more than wearing a cross or placing a bumper sticker on your car. Rather, wearing your witness is about doing those same things *with intention* so that they will give you the opportunity to bear witness to the change God has worked in your life. In that respect, crosses, bracelets, catchy phrases, bumper stickers, your Bible, or even tattoos (read of Jesus' tattoo in Revelation 19:16) can be used with the intention to show your identity as a believer. Not only do these remind you of who you are, but they can be part of the groundswell of believers in another person's social network to lower the threshold for them to make the decision to believe. An act of care or love or concern can show your genuine, sincere faith to a world that otherwise would have no witness. The first three centuries of Christianity remind us of this. It was genuine Christianity beyond mere slogans that persuaded people of the life-changing power of Jesus the King.

CHAPTER 15—WHEN MISSIONS WILL CEASE

#OurMissionGoesOn

Did Benjamin Franklin carve his name in any trees as a youth? I don't assume that was a rite of passage for future printers in his day, but I do assume he would have been like so many other youths who desired to make their mark for ages to come. Had Ben Franklin lived in Wisconsin, he might have made his mark in a tree now known as The Queen. In 1711, when Ben Franklin was only five years old, The Queen would have been just an acorn deposited near Dousman and forgotten by some absent-minded squirrel.

Nonetheless, the tiny acorn packed with carbohydrates, protein, and fat would begin a transformation from a pungent tasting seed into a mammoth Burr Oak tree that would become the fourth-largest tree of its kind in the world.[75] Today, the tree stands over six stories high. Its trunk is nearly seven meters in circumference, and care is taken not to trim or cut the tree so

---

75 "The Thickest, Tallest, and Oldest Trees in Wisconsin," The Thickest, Tallest, and Oldest Trees in Wisconsin (Monumental Trees), accessed June 21, 2022, https://www.monumentaltrees.com/en/records/usa/wisconsin/.

that no disease might be introduced by a saw or knife blade.[76] Initials won't be carved in this tree, to be sure.

Could this enormous tree be called an acorn? Should it still be considered a nut? After all, it was, indeed, an acorn in 1711, and without that stage of its life, The Queen would not exist today. Considering that acorns are a puny one to four cm in size, The Queen certainly breaks the mold and does not fit the definition of an acorn. Perhaps in the spring of 1711, its story would have been different. It would have made its start as a fruit from an even older oak, but not one directly above it, considering that acorns rarely get enough light for germination under their parent trees.

With the help of the aforementioned amnesiac squirrel, the acorn evidently found its permanent home in loose, nutrient-rich soil. Even with that assistance, it lay dormant, drying in the cold Wisconsin winter until it reached a moisture content of forty-four percent. After this point, it needed constant moist-but-not-wet conditions for no less than thirty to sixty days before breaking out of its acorn shell in the germination process.

At last, The Queen has been transformed from an acorn to an oak tree. Can this acorn be recognized at all in the majestic oak? Does the tree bear any resemblance to the acorn whatsoever? In some way, though, even a child knows this mighty oak is from a tiny acorn. It doesn't have to look like a big acorn to be from an acorn. Something about the substance of the tree carries its evident identity of an acorn transformed into an oak.

76 Chelsey Lewis, "Wisconsin's Biggest Bur Oak Is More than 300 Years Old, And You Can Only See It During a Special Event in October," Journal Sentinel (Milwaukee Journal Sentinel, September 12, 2019), https://www.jsonline.com/story/travel/wisconsin/day-out/2019/09/12/visit-wisconsins-biggest-bur-oak-which-more-than-300-years-old-oaktober-fest/2221630001/.

Post-1953, with the DNA model from Francis Crick, we might say that the acorn and oak have common deoxyribonucleic acid, as well as that rolls off the tongue. Even so, Ben Franklin in the 1700s would have been as correct as we are in identifying it as an oak tree. Yet, had he planted the acorn himself, he would not have been able to fathom the forty-five million acorns this single tree would produce over the next 300 years. Without a doubt, this tree has been through a grand metamorphosis.

The Apostle Paul describes a similar incredible, unfathomable transformation we each will make as followers of Jesus when he writes,

> *But someone will say, "How are the dead raised? With what kind of body will they come?" Fool! What you sow will not come to life unless it dies. And what you sow is not the body that is to be, but a bare seed—perhaps of wheat or something else. But God gives it a body just as he planned, and to each of the seeds a body of its own. All flesh is not the same: People have one flesh, animals have another, birds and fish another. And there are heavenly bodies and earthly bodies. The glory of the heavenly body is one sort and the earthly another. There is one glory of the sun, and another glory of the moon and another glory of the stars, for star differs from star in glory. It is the same with the resurrection of the dead. What is sown is perishable, what is raised is imperishable. It is sown in dishonor, it is raised in glory; it is sown in weakness, it is raised in power; it is sown a natural body, it is raised a spiritual body. If there is a natural body, there is also a spiritual body. So*

also it is written, "The first man, Adam, became a living person"; the last Adam became a life-giving spirit. However, the spiritual did not come first, but the natural, and then the spiritual. The first man is from the earth, made of dust; the second man is from heaven. Like the one made of dust, so too are those made of dust, and like the one from heaven, so too those who are heavenly. And just as we have borne the image of the man of dust, let us also bear the image of the man of heaven.

1 Corinthians 15:35–49

Whether that transformation will come through death or rapture, all believers will go through it. Our bodies will, at one point, be physical and, later, spiritual. Can we envision what those bodies will look like, act like, feel like, or do from what we know of our present bodies? Scripture gives us some clues, but largely, we will have to experience it. We need to be transformed.

One of the clues we have is from the spiritual body Jesus received after his resurrection. We can surmise that we will be recognizable despite all of the changes we will undergo (Luke 24:39). That being said, our bodies will be substantially different and will not operate according to the same laws (John 20:19).

In the same way that our bodies will be transformed, our goal, purpose, aim—our *telos*—will be transformed. In some sense, it will remain recognizably the same, while in another sense, it will be made new with many differences.

To be sure, one of the most evident changes will be the complete absence of evangelism and missions. What has preoccupied us for millennia will be no longer. What has been considered foremost won't even register as an afterthought. Jesus' final command of Acts 1:8 and his previous commission of Matthew 28:19–20 will be made redundant.

What many people see as the Great Commission is encapsulated in these few words from Matthew 28:19: "*Going, therefore, make disciples*" (author's translation). Indeed, this passage overshadows the concept of "missions" for some people so that they mistakenly only see cross-cultural missions as the mission of God's people. In linguistics, this is referred to as "synecdoche" or "a part is put for the whole."[77] "Missions," which is a part of our purpose, is erroneously put forward as the totality of our mission or purpose. Although our mission necessarily entails cross-cultural missions, our mission is larger than missions. Indeed, missions alone is not our mission.

Rather, when we think of our mission and even Great Commission work, we should think of making disciples while doing all of the other things the people of God do like creation care, blessing, justice, righteousness, humility, mercy, freedom, care for widows and orphans, and even work. These are the substance that show what a world is like when people follow God. As such, we are to "*make disciples*" while "*going*" about all of those other activities that comprise our mission as people made in the image of God.

The Beginning and End of Missions

As detailed earlier, there is a distinct difference between mission as a goal, purpose, or aim and mission as an activity to achieve a goal, purpose, or aim. Many missions (activities) are used to accomplish a mission (goal). Specifically, the cross-cultural missionary activity of going to all the nations with the Gospel is but one of the activities the Lord commands us to do in order to

77 Merriam Webster, "Synecdoche Definition & Meaning," Merriam-Webster (Merriam-Webster), accessed April 23, 2022, https://www.merriam-webster.com/dictionary/synecdoche.

achieve our mission, that is, our created purpose.

To illustrate this, consider that there was a time when cross-cultural missions and proclamation of the Gospel did not exist. Specifically, this was the time when people did not need to call on the name of the Lord since everyone knew the Lord: "*To Seth also a son was born, and he called his name Enosh. At that time people began to call upon the name of the LORD*" (Genesis 4:26, ESV). Everyone knew the Lord directly or knew someone who had seen and heard and talked to the Lord directly. There was no need to "believe" on the Lord. There was no need to trust someone else's account because people had direct experience of knowing the Lord.

Moreover, there will be a time again when there will be no need for people to urge one another to believe on the Lord. The Lord will be personally seen and known by all:

> *"People will no longer need to teach their neighbors and relatives to know me. For all of them, from the least important to the most important, will know me," says the Lord. "For I will forgive their sin and will no longer call to mind the wrong they have done."*
>
> *Jeremiah 31:34*

Jeremiah foreshadows this pronouncement with a description of the character and desire of these people,

> *"I will give them the desire to acknowledge that I am the Lord. I will be their God and they will be my people. For they will wholeheartedly return*

to me."

(24:7)

This notion is not merely an Old Testament concept of Jeremiah alone, but it is picked up on and reiterated with force by the author of Hebrews,

> *And there will be no need at all for each one to teach his countryman or each one to teach his brother saying, 'Know the Lord,' since they will all know me, from the least to the greatest.*
>
> *(8:11)*

It is clear, then, that there was a time when "missions" did not exist. Among family members or neighbors or distant nations, there was no need for the activity of sending people to tell others about the Lord.

Coupled with that conclusion, there will be a time when "missions" will not exist. Among family members or neighbors or distant nations, there will be no need for the activity of sending people to tell others about the Lord.

All that being said, the mission of God's people endures. The mission of God's people is to represent God in the world. This has not ceased since the creation of humanity, and it will not cease through all eternity.

Bearing the image of God, then, should be the first thing that comes to mind when we ask the question, "What is the mission of God's people?" By doing these things, that is, carrying out our creation/cultural mandate, we fulfill the mission of God's people, namely, to represent him in the world.

Got Plans for the Next Billion Years?

Remembering things is difficult, especially things from the past. I suppose that is one of the drawbacks of being finite. We are challenged in our mental capacity to recall. Likewise, we are challenged in our finitude to project.

For instance, how many of us have ever counted anything to one thousand? Even rattling off numbers in games as children, most of us likely gave up counting before reaching 1000, but how about 10,000 or 100,000 or one million? We may work with large numbers in mathematics, but do we really have a concept of what a billion is?

In a very real sense, we cannot grasp the idea of living for a billion years. We just don't know what that will be like. Even speculating might seem frivolous. Just as Ben Franklin would have had difficulty comprehending that one acorn in 1711 would yield forty-five million acorns in 300 years, we have difficulty comprehending eternal, infinite years with the Savior.

That being the case, it is helpful to follow Ben Franklin in thinking about seeds. What seeds are being planted through our lives in these few seventy or eighty years we might have that will last through eternity?

Many people have the notion that eternity will be spent as a church worship service. Perhaps, we will sit on clouds playing harps and singing to God on his throne forever. I've never seen a church service quite like that, but we can safely dispense with the unbiblical notion of cherubs on clouds playing harps. But what about an eternal worship service? Will we simply sit in church singing *Amazing Grace* for the remainder of all time?

In one sense, we will live for all eternity in a worship service of sorts. The Apostle John writes,

> *Now I saw no temple in the city, because the Lord God—the All-Powerful—and the Lamb are its temple. The city does not need the sun or the moon to shine on it, because the glory of God lights it up, and its lamp is the Lamb. The nations will walk by its light and the kings of the earth will bring their grandeur into it.*
>
> *Revelation 21:22–24*

Of course, saying there will be no temple is not to say that there will be no need for worship, but rather that the Lord God and the Lamb will be present directly so that there will be no need of a temple. All of life will be lived in worship. Worship will be continual in all that we do, so there will be no need for a special place to go to worship, such as a temple would provide, and there will not be a special time or special activity of worship.

Revelation 21 highlights that the holy city, the New Jerusalem, will descend from heaven:

> *So he took me away in the Spirit to a huge, majestic mountain and showed me the holy city, Jerusalem, descending out of heaven from God. The city possesses the glory of God; its brilliance is like a precious jewel, like a stone of crystal-clear jasper. It has a massive, high wall with twelve gates, with twelve angels at the gates, and the names of the twelve tribes of the nation of Israel are written on the gates. There are three gates on*

the east side, three gates on the north side, three gates on the south side and three gates on the west side. The wall of the city has twelve foundations, and on them are the twelve names of the twelve apostles of the Lamb. The angel who spoke to me had a golden measuring rod with which to measure the city and its foundation stones and wall. Now the city is laid out as a square, its length and width the same. He measured the city with the measuring rod at fourteen hundred miles (its length and width and height are equal).

vv. 10–16

The fact can't be ignored that a city is a cultural good itself and necessitates work to maintain and operate. Considering the immense size of this city with its gates, its walls, and foundations, it will take herculean effort to maintain and operate this city. Additionally, nations will continue to exist with their kings bringing their grandeur to present to the Lord in the city. All of this indicates ongoing culture, ongoing activity, and ongoing work. Far from being a celestial haven of cherubs merely singing and playing harps, the picture of heaven we have from Scripture is a bustling city full of life, innovation, and design. One might even say heaven will be filled with art, order, and care.

Regarding the cultural artifact of kings and nations, author Andy Crouch notes, "Just as the king of a nation, in the biblical mind, is the representative of an entire *ethnos* or people, the glory of a nation is simply its greatest and most distinctive cultural achievement…"[78]

Our role as God's image-bearers will carry on through the transformation from this life to eternity. To be sure, each cultural good

78 Andy Crouch, *Culture Making: Recovering Our Creative Calling* (Downers Grove, IL: Intervarsity Press, 2013), 243.

we might bring that represents the grandeur of kings will have gone through a sort of radical transformation. Though France was known for its use of the guillotine and the USSR was known for the AK-47 and the US for its nuclear bombs, these innovations certainly will not be the distinguishing characteristics of these nations where there is no death, and every tear will be wiped away. All of our very best will still fall short and still go through a clear transformation. Crouch poses a question to this effect:

> *So it's a fascinating exercise to ask about any cultural artifact: can we imagine this making it into the new Jerusalem? What cultural goods represent the "glory and honor" of the many cultural traditions we know? We already have biblical assurance that the ships of Tarshish will be there; perhaps they will share a harbor with an Americas' Cup yacht and a lovingly carved birch bark canoe. My own personal list of "the glory and honor of the nations" would surely include Bach's B Minor Mass, Miles Davis's Kind of Blue and Arvo Pärt's "Spiegel im Spiegel"; green-tea crème brûlée, fish tacos and bulgogi; Moby-Dick and the Odyssey; the iPod and the Mini Cooper. Of course I don't expect any of them to appear without being suitably purified and redeemed, any more than I expect my own resurrected body to be just another unimproved version of my present one. But I will be very surprised if they are not carried in by one or another of the representatives of human culture, for they are part of the glorious best that human beings have made of the twelve-tone scale, the flavors of the natural world, language, the microchip and the internal*

combustion engine. [79]

Randy Alcorn masterfully uses fiction to teach concepts with an eternal perspective on heaven and the afterlife. Listen to this teaching from an angel to a young boy who went to heaven early and consider the way heaven will be a process of discovery and innovation and learning that we were intended to do all along:

> *Did you not also read in Elyon's Book [the Bible] his promise that in coming ages he will continuously reveal to us the incomparable riches of his grace? How then could you expect to know everything there is to know? Or to know immediately everything you will one day know? This would defy the way of process and discovery designed by Elyon for his creatures...*

> *Elyon is the Creator, we are the creatures, and always shall be. Heaven does not make you inhuman. It allows you to become all it means to be human. The Creator knows all, and knows all at once. The creature's knowledge is and always will be both partial and gradual. It will grow continuously throughout eternity.*

Crouch describes his view of innovation and creativity further,

> *...our eternal life in God's recreated world will*

---

79 Andy Crouch, *Culture Making: Recovering Our Creative Calling* (Downers Grove, IL: Intervarsity Press, 2013), 170.

> *be the fulfillment of what God originally asked us to do: cultivating and creating in full and lasting relationship with our Creator. This time, of course, we will not just be tending a garden; we will be sustaining the life of a city, a harmonious human society that has developed all the potentialities hidden in the original creation to their fullest. Culture—redeemed, transformed and permeated by the presence of God—will be the activity of eternity.*[80]

Our cultural investment in heaven will include ongoing skill and insight that we started here on earth through the investment in all of the various aspects of the integral life. We have every indication that we will continue to operate in a society in heaven that has been perfectly redeemed and restored to its original intent.

This conclusion is not unlike that of Anthony Hoekema,

> *In the beginning man was given the so-called cultural mandate—the command to rule over the earth and to develop a God-glorifying culture. Because of man's fall into sin, that cultural mandate has never been carried out in the way God intended. Only on the new earth will it be perfectly and sinlessly fulfilled. Only then shall we be able to rule the earth properly*[81]

At present, we should recognize that gifts are missing in the

---

80 Andy Crouch, *Culture Making: Recovering Our Creative Calling* (Downers Grove, IL: Intervarsity Press, 2013), 173.
81 Randy Alcorn, *Heaven: God's Answers for Your Every Need* (Carol Stream, IL: Tyndale House, 2004), 414.

expression of the Church. We know that things are not as they should be. This is due, of course, to people refusing to use the gifts they have been given or that lack of believers in the Church who would have been gifted but haven't made a profession of faith even to begin the process.

In the New Heaven and New Earth, all of the gifts will be perfectly represented with no sinful disobedience of individuals holding back the gifts they have been given. We will experience the perfect expression of all that the Lord originally intended humanity to be.

As theologian Cornelius Venema says in *The Promise of the Future*,

> *Every legitimate and excellent fruit of human culture will be carried into and contribute to the splendour of life in the new creation. Rather than the new creation being a radically new beginning, in which the excellent and noble fruits of humankind's fulfillment of the cultural mandate are wholly discarded—the new creation will benefit from, and be immensely enriched by, its receiving of these fruits.*[82]

Summary

It can be concluded, then, that our mission is much larger than missions. Indeed, missions itself will become a relic of days past when we see the full expression of our gifts exhibited in the New Heavens and New Earth. There will be no need for missions or evangelism. We will no longer have the burden of applying our

82 Ibid.

innovation and creativity to presenting the Gospel in a way that catches people's attention and communicates the truth in an attractive manner that can be readily understood. Indeed, all of the effort of language learning and translation of the Word of God into the heart languages of the world's people groups will be no more. All of that effort can be applied to its original intended purpose because missions and evangelism will be no more. Even now, it is clear that missions alone is not our mission.

CHAPTER 16—OUR MISSION THROUGH MISSIONS

#GloryAndJoy

Richard was a very handy person to have around camp. Although he was the camp director, he often found himself involved in the work himself, not just directing the work. You would just as readily find him on a backhoe excavating a landscaping plot as you would find him in his office doing paperwork.

One particular day, the filtration pump for the swimming pool failed, and the head of maintenance, Bob, was reading the manual to educate himself on how to fix it. As the camp director, Richard stopped in to check in on Bob's progress because having the pool closed for any length of time was not tenable for the operations of the camp. Seeing that Bob was busy with the manual, Richard leaned over the pump and started to analyze its function by tracing back the pipes into the different cylinders. Bob warned, "Now, don't mess with anything. I'm trying to figure out how it works."

Richard responded, "Bob, I wrote that book!" Shocked at this revelation, Bob turned to the front cover and countered, "Well, your name isn't on it."

Undeterred, Richard explained that a person with a mind like his figured out how to design a pool filtration pump, so he was reverse-engineering this design. He proceeded to fix the pump in spite of Bob's protests.

The main drawback of Richard's approach is time. To be sure, any one of us can cultivate the wherewithal to reverse-engineer the design of a pool filtration pump given enough time. Richard's background as a Green Beret may have given him an edge as "one of the best and brightest," but if we have the time on our hands, anyone can master even the most difficult skill or trade. On the other hand, not all of us have the time to apply to this, so we hire specialists who are seasoned with years of experience on many different types of filtration pumps. Those specialists may have applied themselves to an apprenticeship or achieved journeyman status or craftsman or even master craftsman.

In many specialties, expertise is the preferred skill over ingenuity. An astute engineer who just "figures things out" is admired, but not trusted when it comes to cardiac surgery, for example. The skill of a cardiac surgeon with years of training and board certifications cannot be replaced by Richard's gusto for figuring things out.

Moreover, the ability to get things done, that is, utility, is not the only ability to be esteemed. I once had the motto "Utility, not vanity." My point in living by this was that things should be measured by their usefulness, not by their aesthetic. I saw a great deal of waste in making things beautiful when something much simpler and less expensive could get the job done without the "wasted" time.

In writing *Work of Influence: Principles for Professionals from the Book of Daniel*, I came to a different understanding. More accurately, in reading the book of Exodus, I came to a different understanding. Consider Moses' words in chapter 36:1–3,

So Bezalel and Oholiab and every skilled person in whom the Lord has put skill and ability to know how to do all the work for the service of the sanctuary are to do the work according to all that the Lord has commanded.

Moses summoned Bezalel and Oholiab and every skilled person in whom the Lord had put skill—everyone whose heart stirred him to volunteer to do the work, and they received from Moses all the offerings the Israelites had brought to do the work for the service of the sanctuary, and they still continued to bring him a free will offering each morning.

Of course, my utilitarian nature resonated with the skill that the Lord put in people, but my eyes were opened to a different purpose, namely, beauty. The Lord equipped Bezalel and Oholiab with the mastery of their work for the purpose of building a beautifully ornate structure. The Lord put this skill in them. The Lord enabled them to do their work with the utmost care. The Lord was the one who both benefited from the beautiful craftsmanship that was exhibited and the one who put it there, to begin with.

The work was not about merely getting a job done which probably would have been my inclination in my earlier years. Richard got the job done with his approach. It may not have been the most elegant way, but he got the job done. With Bezalel and Oholiab, the work was about making a contribution to the world through the skill that God himself had put in them.

After having my eyes opened to this reality from Exodus 36, I noticed something similar in Exodus 25 in this instruction from God to Moses:

You must make holy garments for your brother Aaron, for glory and for beauty.

(2)

Again, the command was more than just getting a job done. The Lord didn't say, "Yeah, I suppose you should make some clothes for Aaron and his sons. Denim is probably the most durable. Use that." The craftsmanship that the Lord required was nothing short of glorious and beautiful.

By every description we have, heaven will be incredibly ornate. The design of the walls and the gates of pearls will be for glory and for beauty. Indeed, the most beautiful translucent gold will be used as asphalt for the streets in the New Jerusalem. What do we use for streets in this world? We use cheap stone as aggregate mixed with oil and tar to make it conform to the shape of the potholes to fill. In other words, we recognize that our roads are virtually disposable and will be replaced every five to ten years, so we use the cheapest material possible.

On the other hand, gold represents the most costly metal at our disposal. It is so valuable that it is measured and sold by the ounce. Our very best and most ornate materials in this world will barely find their use as the most common materials to be trodden under foot in the next world.

Preparing for What's Ahead

The Apostle Paul presents an unbroken chain about the challenging topic of predestination in Romans 8:28–30,

> *And we know that all things work together for good for those who love God, who are called according to his purpose, because those whom he foreknew he also predestined to be conformed to the image of his Son, that his Son would be the firstborn among many brothers and sisters. And those he predestined, he also called; and those he called, he also justified; and those he justified, he also glorified.*

Some people struggle with predestination, particularly in regard to the responsibility of people to walk through the steps involved in that predestination. For instance, why should I pray for my father to come to faith? God has already predestined him either to heaven or to hell. He already knows the outcome, so why pray?

Romans 8 answers this for us in the same way that it answers for us the purpose of these trying, difficult years on earth. Indeed, God foreknew, predestined, called, justified, and glorified all those who would believe. Being outside of time, he can't help but foreknow and predestine those who will in time be called, justified, and glorified. For us, we must see this as a series of sequential events, but for God, he sees all of them at once.

The point where this becomes so practical is that God also sees the preaching and the prayers and sacrificial giving and language learning and the travel and the witness and the suffering and the martyrdom of faithful witnesses to call those who will be justified and glorified. Indeed, as Paul writes later,

> *How are they to call on one they have not believed in? And how are they to believe in one they have not heard of? And how are they to hear without someone preaching to them?*
>
> Romans 10:14

The physician who sacrificially gives thousands of dollars to send a missionary family to Bangladesh not only serves God through her care for her patients. Her integral life extends to the supporting effort of calling Bangladeshis to Jesus, giving them an opportunity to respond to the Gospel that they would not have had. God ordains that service of generosity to him just as he ordains healing through cardiac surgery.

Should you pray even though God already knows the outcome? Without a doubt. God ordains the prayer just as well as he ordains the outcome. It is in prayer that we are drawn closer to the mind and heart of God. In a very real sense, we pray because our prayer changes us.

Should you go through this painful, difficult, stressful life even though your place in heaven is already secured? Without a doubt. God ordains this life just as he ordains its outcome. This life prepares us for eternity with him.

Ballooning Capacity for the Savior

My father resisted faith in Jesus for decades. I appealed to him often. I reasoned with him repeatedly. My sister, my half-brother, my half-sister all came to profess faith in Jesus, but my father resisted.

Unfortunately, my father was a casualty of COVID-19. I received word through my sister that his organs were shutting down, and he had, perhaps, hours or days to live. My half-brother was called home from Naval service in Japan and started a Facetime call with me from my father's hospital room.

Again, I reasoned with my father demonstrating that sin against an infinitely good God cannot be compensated by finite creatures. We need to trust Jesus who made an infinite sacrifice to atone for our sin.

In perhaps some of the most beautiful words I've ever heard, my father said, "I agree." I had the privilege of praying with him that day as he placed his trust in Jesus.

My father died four days later. That conversation was one of the last few lucid conversations he had. It was one of the last opportunities he had to consciously place his trust in the Savior. Like the criminal on the cross who placed his trust in Jesus at the last possible moment, I believe I will see my father in heaven.

That being said, how will my father's experience in heaven differ from Phyllis Meyer who led me to faith after many decades of following the Lord? It's reasonable to surmise that my father is experiencing a sense of loss that he didn't make this decision sooner. Now that he is enjoying the presence of the Savior, he is likely wondering why he was so foolish not to begin the relationship earlier and enjoy the delights of the Savior more during his life on earth.

Jonathan Edwards wrote,

> *There are different degrees of happiness and glory in heaven. . .Christ tells us that he who gives a cup of cold water unto a disciple in the name of*

> *a disciple, shall in no wise lose his reward. But this could not be true, if a person should have no greater reward for doing many good works than if he did but few. It will be no damp to the happiness of those who have lower degrees of happiness and glory, that there are others advanced in glory above them: for all shall be perfectly happy, every one shall be perfectly satisfied. Every vessel that is cast into this ocean of happiness is full, though there are some vessels far larger than others...* [83]

Edwards is careful to note that all believers in heaven will be full of joy, but he builds on this idea elsewhere,

> *The saints are like so many vessels of different sizes cast into a sea of happiness where every vessel is full: this is eternal life, for a man ever to have his capacity filled. But after all 'tis left to God's sovereign pleasure, 'tis his prerogative to determine the largeness of the vessel.*[84]

I liken this idea of our vessels to balloons. Each of our balloons will be full, but there will be some balloons larger than others. Nonetheless, smaller balloons will still have full happiness (that is, "It will be no damp to the happiness of those who have lower degrees of happiness and glory") even though there will be larger balloons.

---

83 Jonathan Edwards, "Works of Jonathan Edwards, Volume Two," Jonathan Edwards: Works of Jonathan Edwards, Volume Two (Christian Classics Ethereal Library), accessed June 3, 2021, https://www.ccel.org/ccel/edwards/works2.xv.viii.html.
84 Randy Alcorn, *Heaven: God's Answers for Your Every Need* (Carol Stream, IL: Tyndale House, 2004), 369.

Simply put, the good that we do in this life increases our capacity for joy in the next life. My father's balloon is full. He is fully satisfied in heaven. His happiness is not diminished because he looks around and sees larger balloons.

Even so, Phyllis Meyer enjoys a larger balloon. Her reward of happiness and joy with Jesus is greater because she built greater capacity through decades of service to the Lord. She nurtured and cared for that relationship with her Savior for the majority of her life. In the words of Jonathan Edwards, "[She] shall in no wise lose [her] reward."

The purpose of this life and serving the Lord to the fullest measure is to increase our capacity to enjoy the Savior for eternity. We do this by representing our Creator's image through art, order, and care.

Perpetual Students

Chapter 15 demonstrates how heaven will be filled with culture-making and endless innovation and exploration as the kings of the nations bring the best of their redeemed cultural goods to present before the Lord. Just as we do now, we take the raw material of the cultural goods we are given, and we make something of the world. In the New Jerusalem, we will take the raw materials of the radically transformed cultural goods we are given, and we will make something of the world.

Randy Alcorn notes of our creation,

> *God's intention for humans was that we would occupy the whole Earth and reign over it. This dominion would produce God-exalting societies in which we would exercise the creativity, imag-*

ination, intellect, and skills befitting beings created in God's image, thereby manifesting his attributes.

Culture encompasses commerce, the arts, sciences, athletics—anything and everything that God-empowered, creative human minds can conceive and strong human bodies can implement. In The King of the Earth, theologian Erich Sauer writes of the phrase in Genesis 1:26, "let them have dominion": "These words plainly declare the vocation of the whole human race to rule. They also call him to progressive growth in culture. Far from being something in conflict with God, cultural achievements are an essential attribute of the nobility of man as he possessed it in Paradise. Inventions and discoveries, the sciences and the arts, refinement and ennobling, in short, the advance of the human mind, are throughout the will of God. They are the taking possession of the earth by the royal human race (Genesis 1:28), the performance of a commission, imposed by the Creator, by God's ennobled servants, a God-appointed ruler's service for the blessing of this earthly realm."

This reigning, expanding, culture-enriching purpose of God for mankind on Earth was never revoked or abandoned.[85]

85 Randy Alcorn, *Heaven: God's Answers for Your Every Need* (Carol Stream, IL: Tyndale House, 2004), 226-227.

We will continue to do what we were created to do, although we will do it with pure, transformed minds and bodies to do it fully and completely for God's glory. We will continually learn, grow, innovate, produce, care for, and design in the New Creation. Essentially, we will become perpetual students learning and loving the Lord more each moment for all eternity.

Summary

Far from singing cherubs on floating clouds, the New Jerusalem will be a continual bustle of joyful, productive activity using all of the best we have to offer of this world in a new and transformed manner. We will continue to exercise our roles of art, order, and care to maximize the image of God we reflect while doing it without the hindrance of sinful minds and actions that now entangle us. This gives us purpose and joy not only then, but now as we build our capacity to enjoy the Savior more for eternity.

CONCLUSION

The Integral Life is fundamentally about living a whole, complete life with purpose. What is the purpose of life? What have we been called to do in the world? What will we do for eternity? What is the underlying theme that connects our original created purpose with our lives in this sinful world and our ultimate destiny as followers of Jesus?

The Bible's given reason for our creation is to bear the image of God throughout creation. In bearing his image, we model what he, himself, did in creation, namely, art, order, and care. Fulfilling these roles of creator, curator, and cultivator gives us the opportunity to glorify God through all that we do, whether that is through marriage, family, friendship, work, Church, or community.

An easy way to think of this is through the Telos Tower which represents a foundation for all of life built on the commission we received at the creation of Adam and Eve.

One of the primary challenges in thinking through a book that spans from creation to the New Jerusalem is how to apply it. We might think through these pieces logically just as the Philippian jailer thought through the words of the songs that Paul and Silas sang in Acts 16. This indirect witness of Paul and Silas was absorbed by the jailer who wondered how they could sing with such joy while going through such suffering. It simply made him curious.

For that Philippian jailer, his teachable moment came after an earthquake that threw open the doors of the prison. Thinking that the prisoners had escaped and he would receive torture from the Roman Praetorium, he chose suicide instead. As he was about to fall on his sword, Paul and Silas cried out that they were all there and he should not harm himself.

Again, he was astonished at them not just because of their joy through suffering, but because they did not seize on the opportunity to escape. The wonder was too much to keep within any longer. "Sirs, what must I do to be saved?" (Acts 16:30)

What will you do with the truth you have been presented in this book? How will it change your day-to-day life? As you recognize the sovereignty of God in choosing you for salvation, what will you do in response to this great gift?

Let me offer a response for your consideration. Focus each day around these two questions,

1. What will I do today to prepare for eternity?
2. What will I do today to support those around me?

The first question encompasses an ever-deepening love for the Savior. This life is not merely a means to the end of getting to heaven. Your relationship with your loving Savior begins now. What are you doing today to know God more and love God more? What capacity are you building to water the acorn of your life before its ultimate transformation?

The renewed focus that the integral life offers is a whole, complete life. This is in opposition to a fractured, compartmentalized life. In the integral life, you are not working at your job to put food on the table. In a very real way, you are fulfilling your created calling as a creator, curator, and cultivator. You are deepening your intimacy with the One who made you.

You are not caring for your spouse just because marriage is a culturally acceptable means of living. You are learning more of the intimacy with the Savior through the understanding of intimacy in your marriage. You are fulfilling your created calling.

"What will I do today to support those around me?" This is *the integral life*. In answering this question you are recognizing the irreplaceable impact you have as an individual in society. You are not an automaton of a communist society that is programmed to fill a slot of efficient production. You have a purpose in making a unique contribution to those in your family, social network, Church, and community. Your job, as well, is not merely a means of knowing and serving the Savior, but it is a means of serving and supporting those around you.

When we consider life from this perspective, we see our created calling to represent the image of God in the world. The integral life guards us from compartmentalizing our faith-based life apart from our recreational life or our civic life or our occupational life or our family life or our social life. We are whole beings made to serve the one true Creator God with our whole lives. As the Apostle Paul preached,

> *The God who made the world and everything in it, who is Lord of heaven and earth, does not live in temples made by human hands, nor is he served by human hands, as if he needed anything, because he himself gives life and breath and everything to everyone. From one man he made every nation of the human race to inhabit the entire earth, determining their set times and the fixed limits of the places where they would live, so that they would search for God and perhaps grope around for him and find him, though he is not far*

from each one of us.

Acts 17:24–27

May we live our lives with complete passion and purpose for God through all eternity.

εἰς τὴν δόξαν τοῦ θεοῦ

eis ten doxan tou theou

"To the glory of God"

BIBLIOGRAPHY

Alcorn, Randy C. *Deadline*. Sisters, OR: Multnomah Books, 1994.

Alcorn, Randy. *Heaven: God's Answers for Your Every Need*. Carol Stream, IL: Tyndale House, 2004.

Alone in the Wilderness. DVD. United States: Bob Swerer Productions, 2003.

Bakke, Odd Magne. When Children Became People: The Birth of Childhood in Early Christianity. Minneapolis, MN: Fortress Press, 2007.

Bazelon, Emily. "The Place of Women on the Court." The New York Times. The New York Times, July 7, 2009. https://www.nytimes.com/2009/07/12/magazine/12ginsburg-t.html.

Bohon, Dave. "Broken Homes in the United States Are at Alarming Level, Study Finds." The New American, November 23, 2011. https://www.thenewamerican.com/culture/family/item/829-broken-homes-in-the-united-states-are-at-alarming-level-study-finds.

Chalmers, Vanessa. "150,000 Brits Will Die during Coronavirus Pandemic through Domestic Violence and Suicides." Daily Mail Online. Associated Newspapers, April 10, 2020. https://www.dailymail.co.uk/news/article-8207783/150-000-Brits-die-coronavirus-pandemic-domestic-violence-suicides.html.

Chandler, Matt, and Jared Wilson. *The Explicit Gospel.* Wheaton, IL: Crossway Books, 2014.

Collins, Francis S. The Language of God: A Scientist Presents Evidence for Belief. New York, NY: Simon & Schuster, 2006.

Cross, David. Work of Influence: Principles for Professionals from the Book of Daniel. 2nd ed. Burlington, WI: Professionals Global, 2020.

Crouch, Andy. *Culture Making: Recovering Our Creative Calling.* Downers Grove, IL: Intervarsity Press, 2013.

Curtis, Wayne. And a Bottle of Rum: A History of the New World in Ten Cocktails. New York, NY: Broadway Books, 2018.

Dalfonzo, Gina. "C. S. Lewis's Joy in Marriage." Christianity-Today.com. Christianity Today, October 8, 2013. https://www.christianitytoday.com/ct/2013/october-web-only/cs-lewis-joy-in-marriage.html.

De La Mora, Brittni. "Brittni De La Mora." Love Always Ministries. Accessed April 23, 2022. https://www.lovealwaysministries.com/brittnidelamora.

DeYoung, Kevin, and Greg Gilbert. What Is the Mission of the Church?: Making Sense of Social Justice, Shalom, and the Great Commission. Wheaton, IL: Crossway, 2011.

Dickson, EJ. "Coronavirus Is Wreaking Havoc on Our Mental Health." Rolling Stone. Rolling Stone, March 11, 2020. https://www.rollingstone.com/culture/culture-news/coronavirus-covid-19-mental-health-crisis-961247/.

Dorsett, Lyle W., ed. *The Essential C.S. Lewis.* New York, NY: Collier, 1988.

Douglas, Paul, and Mitch Hescox. Caring for Creation: The

Evangelical's Guide to Climate Change and a Healthy Environment. Minneapolis, MN: Bethany House Publishers, 2016.

Edgar, William. *Created and Creating: A Biblical Theology of Culture*. Downers Grove, IL: IVP Academic, an imprint of InterVarsity Press, 2017.

Edwards, Bradley J., and Brittany Henderson. *Relentless Pursuit: My Fight for the Victims of Jeffrey Epstein*. New York, NY: Gallery Books, 2020.

Edwards, Jonathan. "Works of Jonathan Edwards, Volume Two." Jonathan Edwards: Works of Jonathan Edwards, Volume Two. Christian Classics Ethereal Library. Accessed June 3, 2021. https://www.ccel.org/ccel/edwards/works2.xv.viii.html.

Ferriss, Timothy. The 4-Hour Work Week: Escape the 9-5, Live Anywhere and Join the New Rich. London, England: Vermilion, 2008.

Finkel, Michael. The Stranger in the Woods: The Extraordinary Story of the Last True Hermit. New York, NY: Alfred A. Knopf, 2017.

Foster, Richard J. Freedom of Simplicity: Revised Edition: Finding Harmony in a Complex World. New York, NY: HarperOne, 2010.

Graves, Stephen R. The Gospel Goes to Work: God's Big Canvas of Calling and Renewal. Fayetteville, AR: KJK Inc. Publishing, 2015.

Grudem, Wayne A., and Elliot Grudem. *Christian Beliefs: Twenty Basics Every Christian Should Know*. Grand Rapids, MI: Zondervan, 2005.

Hale, Thomas. Authentic Lives: Overcoming the Problem of Hidden Identity in Outreach to Restrictive Nations. Pasadena,

CA: William Carey Library, 2016.

Joshua Project. "People Group and Great Commission Statistics: Joshua Project." People Group and Great Commission statistics | Joshua Project. Accessed December 10, 2020. https://joshuaproject.net/people_groups/statistics.

Kahane, Howard. Logic and Contemporary Rhetoric the Use of Reason in Everyday Life. Belmont, CA: Wadsworth, 1992.

Keller, Timothy, and Katherine Leary Alsdorf. *Every Good Endeavor: Connecting Your Work to God's Work*. New York, NY: Penguin Books, an imprint of Penguin Random House, 2014.

King, Martin L. "If a Man Is Called to Be a Street Sweeper." Goodreads. Goodreads. Accessed October 31, 2019. https://www.goodreads.com/quotes/21045-if-a-man-is-called-to-be-a-street-sweeper.

Lewis, Chelsey. "Wisconsin's Biggest Bur Oak Is More than 300 Years Old, And You Can Only See It During a Special Event in October." Journal Sentinel. Milwaukee Journal Sentinel, September 12, 2019. https://www.jsonline.com/story/travel/wisconsin/day-out/2019/09/12/visit-wisconsins-biggest-bur-oak-which-more-than-300-years-old-oaktober-fest/2221630001/.

Lewis, Clive Staples. *The Four Loves*. San Francisco, CA: HarperCollins, 2017.

Little, Benerson. *The Golden Age of Piracy: The Truth Behind Pirate Myths*. New York, NY: Skyhorse Publishing, 2016.

Mansfield, Stephen. *Building Your Band of Brothers*. Pennsauken, NJ: BookBaby, 2017.

McKay, Brett. Building Your Band of Brothers. Other. *Art of Manliness*, January 31, 2017. https://www.artofmanliness.com/articles/podcast-274-building-band-brothers/.

McKinley, Kathryn. "How the Rich Reacted to the Bubonic Plague Has Eerie Similarities to Today's Pandemic." The Conversation, April 25, 2021. https://theconversation.com/how-the-rich-reacted-to-the-bubonic-plague-has-eerie-similarities-to-todays-pandemic-135925.

Pearcey, Nancy. Love Thy Body: Answering Hard Questions about Life and Sexuality. Grand Rapids, MI: Baker Books, 2019.

Pearcey, Nancy. Total Truth: Liberating Christianity from Its Cultural Captivity. Wheaton, IL: Crossway Books, 2008.

Pfeiffer, Charles F., Howard Frederic Vos, and John Rea. *The Wycliffe Bible Encyclopedia*. Chicago, IL: Moody Press, 1975.

Phillips, Richard D. *The Masculine Mandate: God's Calling to Men*. Sanford, FL: Reformation Trust Publishing, 2016.

Piper, John. "Why Is Homosexuality Wrong?" Desiring God. Accessed April 29, 2019. https://www.desiringgod.org/interviews/why-is-homosexuality-wrong.

Ravenhill, Leonard. *Why Revival Tarries*. Bloomington, MN: Bethany House Publishers, 2004.

Ronayne, Kathleen. "California Governor Issues Statewide Stay-at-Home Order." WJXT. WJXT News4JAX, March 20, 2020. https://www.news4jax.com/news/local/2020/03/20/california-governor-orders-statewide-stay-at-home-order.

Salo, Jackie. "Nobel Prize Winner: Coronavirus Lockdowns Cost Lives Instead of Saving Them." New York Post. New York Post, May 26, 2020. https://nypost.com/2020/05/26/nobel-prize-winner-coronavirus-lockdowns-saved-no-lives/amp/.

Sanders, Richard. If a Pirate I Must Be... The True Story of "Black Bart," King of the Caribbean Pirates. New York, NY: Skyhorse, 2007.

Scott, Andrew. *Scatter: Go Therefore and Take Your Job With You.* Chicago, IL: Moody Publishing, 2016.

Smith, Oswald J. "Why Should Anyone Hear the Gospel Twice before Everyone Has Heard It Once?" The Passion for Souls. Accessed April 23, 2022. https://eending-joernaal.webflow.io/blog/why-should-anyone-hear-the-gospel-twice-before-every-one-has-heard-it-once.

Spitters, Denny, and Matthew Ellison. *When Everything Is Missions*. Orlando, FL: Bottomline Media, 2017.

Stark, Rodney. *Cities of God: Christianizing the Urban Empire.* San Francisco, CA: Harper Collins, 2006.

Stark, Rodney. The Rise of Christianity: How the Obscure, Marginal Jesus Movement Became the Dominant Religious Force in the Western World in a Few Centuries. San Francisco, CA: Harper Collins Publishers, 1997.

Stumpf, Samuel Enoch. *Philosophy: History & Problems.* New York, NY: McGrawHill, 1989.

The Thickest, Tallest, and Oldest Trees in Wisconsin. Monumental Trees. Accessed June 21, 2022. https://www.monumentaltrees.com/en/records/usa/wisconsin/.

Thompson, Derek. "Workism Is Making Americans Miserable." *The Atlantic*, February 24, 2019.

Turek, Frank. Dr. Dan and Hope. Other. *Cross Examined.* Frank Turek, April 4, 2020. https://subsplash.com/crossexamined/media/mi/+6zywmjw.

Webster, Merriam. "Synecdoche Definition & Meaning." Merriam-Webster. Merriam-Webster. Accessed April 23, 2022. https://www.merriam-webster.com/dictionary/synecdoche.

Whelchel, Hugh. How Then Should We Work?: Rediscovering the Biblical Doctrine of Work. Bloomington, IN: West Bow Press, 2012.

Wright, Christopher J. H. The Mission of God's People: A Biblical Theology of the Church's Mission. Grand Rapids, MI: Zondervan, 2010.

CPSIA information can be obtained
at www.ICGtesting.com
Printed in the USA
LVHW031057261122
733998LV00004B/29

9 781685 569297